The Buffalo, Ben, and Me

University of Missouri Press   Columbia and London

Todd Parnell

The Buffalo, Ben, and Me

Library of Congress Cataloging-in-Publication Data

Parnell,Todd, 1947–
    The Buffalo, Ben, and me / Todd Parnell.
        p.   cm.
    Summary: "A true story of one man's search for meaning in his life and his efforts
to motivate his son, blending love of family with love of nature in a tale of
transformation. An account of how a trip down a wild river inspired both to a
better use of their lives"—Provided by publisher.
    ISBN 978-0-8262-1752-3 (alk. paper)
    1. Parnell, Todd, 1947– 2. Parnell, Ben (Todd Benjamin), 1981– 3. Fathers
and sons—Arkansas—Biography. 4. Arkansas—Biography. 5. Buffalo River—
Description and travel. I. Title.
    CT275.P354A3 2007
    976.7'053092—dc22
    [B]   2007010394

Designer: Jennifer Cropp
Typesetter: BookComp, Inc.
Printer and binder: Everbest Printing Co. through Four Colour Imports,
                    Louisville, Ky.
Typefaces: Palatino, Raejoi, and Berkeley

To our children, Bart, Patrick, Ben, and Patricia Jean—most special friends to their mother and me.

May you carry these memories with you and share them as you see fit.

More important, may you nurture our two-century-long family love affair with Mother Buffalo and seek to preserve her always—from the ravages of those who don't care, and for the affections of those to come.

The dream and the river were one, inexorably joined, so that they seemed to go on and on, even after both spit me out before dawn, and cast me into that slow waking.

—Harry Middleton, *Rivers of Memory*

We have learned the hard lessons of rivers dammed, ecosystems degraded, and species rendered extinct. We once thought of rivers as a limitless resource, placed on Earth solely for our use . . . We have come to see them as rivers of life.

—John Sawhill, Foreword to *The River Reader*

Before I can live with other folks, I've got to live with myself.

—Harper Lee, *To Kill a Mockingbird*

Given a chance, a child will bring the confusion of the world to the woods, wash it in the creek . . .

—Richard Louv, *Last Child in the Woods*

Contents

Foreword

Whether you love the outdoors or you are a parent looking to reconnect with your kids, or a little of both, this book is a must-read. *The Buffalo, Ben, and Me* chronicles the adventures of Todd Parnell and his son Ben on a memorable journey down the Buffalo River. Ben, a middle-school student, was struggling with an array of learning challenges that left him resentful and underachieving. The trip down the Buffalo River was the result of a casual promise made by Ben's parents to lobby school officials for an unorthodox performance-based reward system. The reward for Ben: twelve adventure-filled days on the Buffalo River with his father.

Against the backdrop of the beautiful Buffalo River in northwest Arkansas, a father searches for his own identity and attempts to help his son gain self-confidence. This is not a mere travel or adventure book. It is, instead, an in-depth look at a man's search for meaning in his life and his efforts to motivate his son.

In *The Buffalo, Ben, and Me*, Todd Parnell showcases his skills as a writer and storyteller. He writes of his love of family and of nature. Far from electronic games, mobile telephones, and the trappings of modern life, parents and kids can connect in unimaginable and wonderful ways and experience what Todd labels "the formative, curative, and redemptive powers of nature."

Jim Baker
Vice President of Missouri State University
and cohost of *OzarksWatch*

Preface

Don't want to be sentimental, but that trip changed my life.

—Benjamin Parnell, June 2, 2003

By the time you reach for this book, Benjamin Parnell will have graduated from the recently renamed Missouri State University. He will have earned a master of science degree, with a biology focus, specializing in stream ecology and fish. Big deal, right? Right.

Ten years ago, young Ben was a struggling student at Wydown Middle School in Clayton, Missouri, seeking meaning and purpose in school or, perhaps more accurately, seeking to avoid both. What follows is a tale of transformation, a testimony to the formative, curative, and redemptive powers of nature. It is a personal story from the heart, written with pride in Ben's long, circuitous journey, which is really just beginning, and with gratitude for the twelve days, ten years ago, that he and I spent together on the Buffalo River in northwest Arkansas—twelve days that provided a focus for the future—for Ben and for me.

What is this Buffalo River of which I speak? She is the longest free-flowing, undammed river west of the Mississippi and simply one of the most beautiful locales on earth. It did not come easy, the undammed part. In the midtwentieth century, the U.S. Army Corps of Engineers set its sights on the nation's remaining free-flowing rivers, with an eye to generating hydroelectric power, creating lakes for recreation and tourism, and controlling flooding. The lower Midwest was a happy hunting ground. The mighty White River was dammed twice in the 1950s and once again in the 1960s. Politicians frothed at the prospect of jobs and economic development. Pork-barrel water projects abounded. Having subdued and conquered the White, the Corps turned to its major tributaries, and the Buffalo River leaped to the top of the list.

In the 1950s, to halt plans for a U.S. Army Corps of Engineers dam was not an easy task. It took a unique coalition of preservationist interests—from the Ozark Society's Kenneth Smith and Neil Compton to Arkansas Senator J. William Fulbright, Supreme Court Justice William O. Douglas, writers and photographers at *Time Magazine* and *National Geographic,* and many other passionate souls along the way—to thwart the powers that were and gain protection for the Buffalo as America's first national river. Richard Nixon, of all people, signed the authorizing legislation in 1972. These few sentences don't do justice to the Buffalo River wars, but Neil Compton's *Battle for the Buffalo River* does. For those in need of an amazing "underdog prevails" kind of tale, Compton's well-researched and heartfelt treatise is inspiring.

Bottom line: I almost lost Benjamin Parnell to mediocrity and boredom, and we almost lost the Buffalo River to greed and avarice. This oversimplification matters to me, because Ben is a son, the river is an inspiration, and both have special places in my heart.

I put this story to paper a decade ago while it was still fresh in my mind. Somehow it seems appropriate to share it in the context of Ben's graduation. I hope it will also help raise awareness for that most noble cause—the protection and preservation of our precious Ozarks water resources and heritage.

As I reread my musings from more than ten years ago, it is painfully clear that this trip hit me as hard as it did Ben—as a wake-up call to life, to what is important, to what is not. How did a rebellious young teen and a middle-aged banker in pursuit of a spark for their floundering attention spans conspire to buck a system keyed to order and predictability? How did the persona of a beautiful river inspire both to a higher and better use of their respective times on this earth? If sharing our personal answers inspires just a few parents and children to embrace the possibilities that nature offers each of us in a world of increasing depersonalization and environmental degradation, the decision to publish will have been a wise one.

Ten years to the week after we began our full Buffalo River adventure together, Ben and I returned from three days on the river. We hadn't thought about it until we were river-bound, on a trip we had planned months earlier. Ben caught a two-and-a-half-pound smallmouth the first day out, not far from where he caught a similar one in 1995. Seems just like yesterday . . . there is a rhythm to it all.

The Buffalo, Ben, and Me

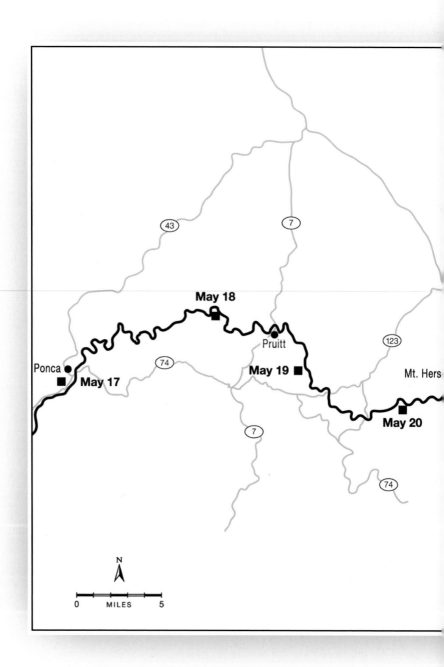

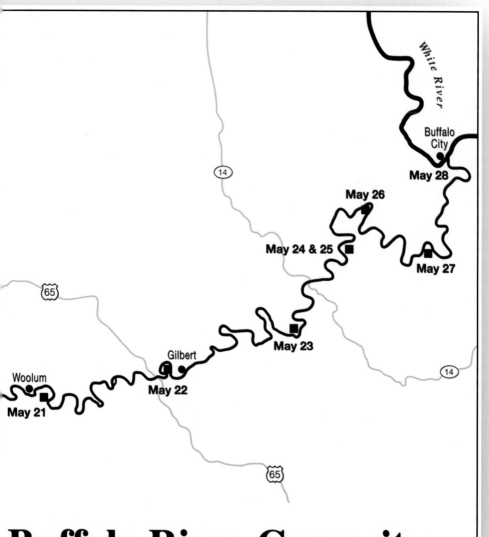

Buffalo River Campsites

Patrick (*left*) and Todd Parnell, putting in at Ponca, Arkansas, on the upper Buffalo River, April 1973.

Below Roark Bluff, April 1973.

April 1973

The Buffalo River, northwest Arkansas, upper section, Ponca to Pruitt. Clean and simple. Put in at the old bridge; several hours later, enjoy a beautiful gravel bar and an evening to rival any. Bluffs at the turn, bluffs in front, and a full moon rising in between. Good food, good wine, and my brother, most of all the companionship of my brother, my friend. We solved problems, some immaterial, some ageless; and, in our exhilaration, innocence, and naïveté we found answers . . . gone tomorrow, but good that night. Little did we realize how gone tomorrow.

Morning brought warning. Our trip had peaked that evening, and we awoke to pending justice, to balance, to offset. The morning sky was red. Not only did we not notice, we cared little and lingered in the certainty of last night's answers.

Evening brought rain, wind, and a minimal dinner. We camped early and low but worried only a little. A new front was coming through, what else?

The "what else" appeared at daybreak the next morning. As we slept in to avoid the heavy rain, a calm collected, then spewed forth

Patrick, seeking to escape rising water.

in a roar. We both sensed a tornado and grappled with the inside corners of the tent, holding them fast in the surrounding chaos. Then came more calm.

We sat in wonder, fear, and awe, perhaps trembling; I don't recall. As we emerged from the tent, we almost stepped in water, brown silty water chock-full of debris. Mother Buffalo was on the rise, and we were in her way. We began to mark her progress with sticks, as we had been taught. It was soon apparent that we were running out of sticks, and out of room. We chose to move on—not that we had much choice. Our campsite was not a good one, with neither elevation nor exit. So down came our tent and all else, to be quickly reloaded in the canoe.

We pushed off into the brown. We caromed down one, maybe two rapids before the waters split: brown to the left, brown to the right. We were swept into trees to the middle and took on a significant amount of water.

We dragged the laden canoe forward to gravel and looked about. We were on an island, with some elevation, but surrounded by silty, sucking current. With a logic we've fortunately yet to replicate, we again set up camp. Water will never reach us here, we reasoned. But as we watched with sinking hearts and hopes, the river crept ever higher and closer. We were exposed for the fools we were.

As the roiling brown foam closed around us, we packed again and tried to push off. We were trapped by rushing water and bending trees. To push out was to swing into more saplings or willows, all alive, all grabbing at our means of escape.

We concluded that our only exit was to swim the canoe away from shore and board her midstream. The April current was shocking to our bodies as we pushed and pulled away. Roots and limbs reached out and clasped our feet with cold, slimy claws. Once clear, we timed our reentry into the canoe so as not to capsize, me bow left, Patrick stern right. It was neither pretty nor safe, but it worked. Our training in earlier years at Kanakuk Kamp in Branson, Missouri, had returned the investment.

Our relief at being free from our island prison was short-lived. New fears crept aboard. Water roiled and sucked around us. Huge pieces of wood raced past or banged our keel. I'll always remember a moment that struck home the gravity of our predicament. At our side a log shot skyward from the cold fury, propelled by the power beneath us, around us. We were clearly at risk.

Afternoon passed to early evening. We needed to get off the raging, ranting object of our previous affection. But we couldn't. There was no way through the trees and bluffs that lined a new channel. We raced by at an alarming pace.

Finally, an eddy formed against a small bluff with an ample rock ledge in front. A whirlpool swirled several yards downstream, but the relative calm beckoned. It was either that or find a tree to tie to as night grew nearer and the water continued to rise.

We pulled over and dragged all up the hillside: canoe, gear, and humbled selves. We set up our tent in a small clearing, nibbled bread as our only meal of the day, and warily watched the water rise below us.

We slept fitfully and rose to find a house farther up the hill. We chose to visit and seek permission to camp until the water retreated. We were greeted by a white German shepherd banging against the inside of the door and then an old lady with withering glare. "Why

The upper Buffalo on the rise, April 1973.

do you fools do this? Don't you know about rivers and spring?" Something like that and more.

And then she softened, perhaps sensing our shaken state, and asked us in. She had lost electric power in the storm yet offered us lunch. We gratefully accepted. As we sat on her porch in poststorm tranquillity and watched the raging river below, she shared her frustration with "the government stealing her land," acreage that had been passed to her through generations. This Buffalo National River malarkey was no more than federal theft, she said. And the ones who wanted to dam up her creek (including the Feds) were no better. She simply wished to be left alone. She would not accept that powerful interests had dictated that it would be one or the other—the Corps of Engineers or the National Park Service, dams or regulation—and that her land would never be the same again. She was grandfathered for her lifetime, but none after her, she explained.

We sat and listened. We felt her anger, her pain, her innocence. We understood her lack of comprehension. The beauty of her valley below, even raging as it was, still sits in a corner of my mind, along with her questions.

A neighbor soon arrived to look after her. We helped him clear the fallen trees that blocked access and heard him tell of seeing the storm pick up a cow and deliver it unharmed to an adjoining field. Strange tale. He also pointed out the path the twister had cleared along the far hillside. It was a sobering sight. We watched as a rescue effort proceeded below with ropes and life jackets, involving several youths in trees. Then the kind neighbor arranged for our safe exit with a phone call my mother will never forget. "Mrs. Parnell, this is (name lost to the years). It's about your boys." Mom says she thrust the phone at Dad, not wanting the rest. She remembers him cracking a smile. It was OK. The search party that family friend Jack Herschend was gathering could stay at home. Mom drove down to pick us up, and ran a tape recorder as we told all during the two-hour ride home. I'm glad she saved the story, for it sounds so surrealistic when replayed.

We wrote the lady and sent her chocolates. We never heard back. She, like our innocence, was gone.

Safety at last, high above the flooded upper Buffalo.

Beginnings   November 1993–April 1995

I'm sitting in my monthly bank board meeting. This is indeed a bank bored meeting of the highest calling. I face the comfortable, wealthy faces all in a row wondering if I'm becoming one myself—comfortable, not wealthy. My mind is wandering and my pen follows, tracing a dream. Mother Buffalo, Ben, and me; just us three.

The Buffalo River has cut and carved the Boston Mountains of northwest Arkansas for eons. Ben and I go way back, too. He's one of my boys, named after his great-grandfather and grandfather before him—all part of this tale. He's an early teen and enamored of nature.

The "me" is a bored banker at a boring board meeting, fifth generation of the trade, perhaps the first so bored. My banker dad didn't run boring meetings. Maybe the trade is not the problem. Whatever.

The dream is to spend days, maybe weeks, together, the Buffalo, Ben, and me. What if Ben and I could float the Buffalo River from stem to stern, from top to bottom, from start to finish, Ponca to White River, all 125 miles of her navigable (with full gear) course, perhaps even putting in a few miles more upstream at Boxley if we caught her just right?

This trip was born in my mind many years ago but took flesh only when Ben grabbed hold. He will soon be gone, out into the world, like his brothers before and his sister to come. Whether to college, adventure, or mundane labor, he will pass beyond my touch before I miss him, leaving remnants of memories and little else. I want him to have this trip to carry with him. I need it to cling to as he leaves my side to pursue dreams and loves.

That's the romantic version. The flip side shows Ben struggling for identity; fighting school, order, and responsibility; talented but lazy; perhaps misplaced in time and space. He is a half stride off, either ahead or behind, his mother likes to say. I am as well, lost in the workplace and looking for a handhold. A career of big banks and bureaucracy has provided income but not inspiration. It shows. What a pair to draw to.

His mother and I worried about Ben. So we decided to try something different for this different lad—a long-term goal, a source of motivation, a bribe, an opportunity to take responsibility for something he valued, a chance to lose it if he failed. He didn't fail, but he came close, and I'm getting ahead of myself.

We began by approaching Ben's principal at Clayton's Wydown Middle School, who was ecstatic about the concept and assured us it fit into the "Wydown model." He saw Ben as "on the edge." It was later determined that Mr. Principal fell off the edge, but that's a sad and different story.

The proposal was this: Ben, who made sixth-grade Ds and Fs, turned nothing in on time, and generally slipped through the cracks because he did not disrupt class, would be given an opportunity to earn one of his life dreams—to float the Buffalo National River in its entirety—if he would establish at least a B average for the remainder of his middle-school career. The kicker was that he would take the trip as a school "project" during the last trimester of his eighth-grade year. The timing was due in part to the simple fact that the river's upper stretches can be floated only in the spring, and in part to our desire to provide a direct linkage to school performance. I would accompany him if he could pull it off. Tough duty for a bored banker. Believe me, I was pulling for him.

As luck would have it, no sooner had Mr. Principal signed off and advised me to start working with Ben's teachers than he was banished to the hinterlands, and later presumably to prison, for sexually abusing one of Ben's classmates. In the chaos that followed, there was little time or room for further discussion of school projects, so we let the matter lie until the beginning of Ben's eighth-grade year. Ben, of course, became an instant scholar, piling A on top of A and soaring to the top echelons of his class. By accident or plan, we had pushed the right button, and Ben had taken control of his destiny.

Come the fall of his eighth-grade year, we regrouped and approached Dr. Nance, the new principal. Her goals in life, she was quick to point out, were to add discipline and consistency to Wydown Middle School. It took vision to find those in a last-trimester float trip, but she did. After all, she was an avid whitewater rafter. She left the final recommendation to Ben's teachers, all of whom endorsed the proposal and its only constraint—Ben had to earn the trip.

Now I was the one with second thoughts. I had crossed the threshold from dream to possibility, had witnessed my wife's willingness to forgo a family vacation for the cause, had cleared a two-month window on my calendar to accommodate the vagaries of weather and water level, and the go/no-go was all Ben's.

Were we putting too much pressure on an early teen? Was this unfair to his fragile ego and adolescent hormones? Would he cheat and lie to succeed? What if he failed?

As I waffled with uncertainty, I had occasion to chat with close family friend from Branson, Jack Herschend. I shared the challenge, the trip, and Ben's sudden turnaround. Jack's eyes lit, then watered. Jack knows the Buffalo, perhaps better than anyone I've met. He knows kids as well. His reaction confirmed for me that we were on the right path. He offered to help with planning, gear, logistics, maps, and whatever else it took. This busy business and civic leader, a cofounder of Branson's Silver Dollar City, grasped the logic and the rationale and put the risk in proper perspective. His reassurances laid my concerns to rest.

Ben didn't fail, and I doubt I ever thought he would. He may be lazy, but buried deep is a quiet resolve.

And then there was Patrick, named after my brother and, before him, my Aunt Pat—and, like her, possessing the soul of an angel. How would he react to all this? Would he resent my spending two weeks away with his younger brother? Would he think I loved him less? Would he carry scars of discrimination and neglect into perpetuity? It seemed unlikely, for Patrick was already beyond us. He was struggling to accommodate parental authority and the insecurity inherent within, but he was already gone—if not in fact, then certainly in spirit.

Not that Patrick hadn't had his fill of the river. As an inductee into the time-honored Parnell tradition of floating by age three, Patrick made his first float in the summer of 1981 on Beaver Creek, a float that resulted in what was quite simply the best day of Smallmouth fishing I have ever experienced: two fish of more than three pounds each within thirty minutes, each released after a kiss from him. For those who don't know, catching a large Smallmouth bass is like catching lightning in a bottle. You will note that I always capitalize *Smallmouth*. They deserve it.

Yet, as Ben and I prepare for this trip, I wonder if Patrick will take offense. Probably. Is it fair not to take him? No. Is it possible to take him now, when he is in the midst of honors English, AP history, studying for his ACTs, and training for the state track meet, where he has a shot at qualifying in the high hurdles? No. Does this sound like a guilty conscience at work? Yes.

And what of my other children, Bart and Patricia Jean, the book-ends of my life, and my wife, Betty, the center?

It comes down to Ben and me. If it is to happen, it has to be us; that's one of life's dictates, fair or not. My concerns aren't easy to slough off, however.

As for the Buffalo River, for those of you who don't know, it flows down from northwest Arkansas's Boston Mountains in an easterly direction into the mighty White River, a major tributary of the Arkansas River, just above the latter's juncture with the Mississippi. A couple of disclaimers here: I am not a world traveler, and I am not a geologist. Still, I'd wager there is no other river like the Buffalo. I once heard Charles Hoessle, director of the St. Louis Zoo, call the river one of the world's uniquely diverse environmental laboratories. Situated on the million-plus-year-old Ozark Plateau, the Buffalo River channel was cut from ancient beds of limestone deposited beneath a long departed shallow sea by free-flowing water whose rare clarity is owed to natural chert gravel filtering and karst topography. That was a mouthful for this rank amateur, and subject to previous disclaimers. Still, until proved wrong, I stand on my previous statement about the river's uniqueness. Like other feeder streams to the upper White River system—the James and Kings rivers; Bull, Swan, and Beaver creeks—the Buffalo flows rich with aquatic life and color. Unlike the others, it cuts through the Boston Mountains and beyond with severe cuts that make gawkers of most men and women. These are among the many reasons the Buffalo is America's first named National River.

As a family, we've shared her many turns and moods over the years. I've experienced her as a youth, in middle-aged stupor, with

The upper Buffalo from Goat Trail, Big Bluff.

Hemmed-in Hollow, upper Buffalo.

my brother, with my mother and brother, with my father and brother, with Betty in newlywed romantic splendor, with the boys on real-men trips, with buddies and their boys—time and time again, always returning. This is my fifth decade of Buffalo River toe dipping, and I'm only in my forties. Somehow the math works, and even if I'm nowhere near being an expert, at least I'm persistent—and adoring. The spring of '95 came early. The countdown accelerated, anticipation burned, and complications multiplied, geometrically. We met the teaching team in early March and agreed on the time frame (two weeks between April 17 and May 31), the specified preparation work (things such as a nature sketching course, a book review of *Buffalo River Country*, identification of several wildlife projects from *The Complete Wilderness Training Book*), and a rough syllabus (journal, water-quality tests, wildlife counts, interviews, math work sheets, and *To Kill a Mockingbird* for English class). It would be a busy trip. We agreed to reconvene the week before departure, which would be timed to water conditions, to finalize Ben's obligations. It was a go!

Complications May 2–17, 1995

Nothing is ever easy, *nothing*. Therefore, why should a two-week, 125-mile voyage into the wilderness for a middle-aged man and his fourteen-year-old son be easy? The complications began just as I thought we were home free. Another truism: you are *never* home free.

With confident complacency, I strode into Ben's classroom on Tuesday, May 2, at about 10:00 a.m. to review the final assignment list with his team of teachers. I even insisted that his mother (and by default his four-year-old sister) join us for the triumphant institutional blessing. I emerged from that meeting a shaken man.

All started as planned, with teachers and checklists and assignments and deadlines. Then the truth leaked, hissing like air from a punctured balloon. Ben had changed since the second-trimester As of a month ago. In math, he didn't pay attention and was near a D. In social studies, he was not passing—*not passing!* In English, he and his teacher were fighting, and he proceeded to provide a demonstration right in front of us that very day. His science teacher sheepishly reported an A.

It was quite obvious—Ben had checked into The Hotel Buffalo a little early. At the peak of his game, at his moment of triumph, he had quit, taken early retirement, and was uncharacteristically obnoxious about it. As I asked him to leave the room and his teachers began to unload, I became nauseous—not angry, nauseous. The Buffalo adventure was melting in front of my eyes. "I don't see how we can go on this trip under these circumstances," I found myself saying.

Ben had made a critical mistake. It could not be condoned. It could not be rewarded.

I scheduled a meeting for that afternoon with Ben's counselor, a man he revered and trusted, always a listener, who could listen no more as I laid out the whole sorry scenario for him. We kicked back and forth the facts, the options, Ben's successes of the previous two years, the risks of letting him make the trip, the risks of not. He suggested that we throw the whole thing back in Ben's lap to save or to lose, granting him full control of his own destiny.

He asked Ben to join us. I told him the trip was off. He had done everything except cross the finish line.

Ben gasped; then he sobbed, hunched over and shaking. He spouted anger, he threatened ("You haven't seen anything yet"), then he softened, and pleaded, and begged, and recounted all of his efforts in pursuit of his dream. Then he sat quietly in his own private turmoil. It was a hard thing for this father to watch.

"What can I do?" he whispered. "I'll do anything," he said.

"Fix it," we responded. "It's all yours."

He started that evening, working long into the night on a personal letter:

Dear Teachers,

I am starting to realize what a horrible mistake I have made. I have treated you with disrespect, like trying to take care of things without thinking. I've been snappy, angry, and bossy, like trying to override the teacher, especially in English, which is totally unacceptable. In math class I have had trouble paying attention, so I have decided to move to an isolated area in the front of the room. I am also free to take any other suggestions the 8th grade math team has. I want to go on this trip more than anything, and all I ask is that you are willing to talk to me about this. I will do anything that is needed either for grades or behavior without any hesitation. I cannot explain my actions of the past few weeks, neither can I blame anybody except myself. All I can offer is my apology and my cooperation with all of you.

Ben Parnell

It was a start. And it was from the heart. He followed up the next morning by meeting personally with each teacher.

There were further problems. On March 27, I had started a new job: new bank, new president and CEO, new chance. For me this would be a long-awaited opportunity to test my personal philosophy, leadership skills, and entrepreneurial ideas and, perhaps most important, to see whether it was me, the boss, or the nature of the business that was the problem. Perhaps a last chance. It didn't matter that it was the smallest bank in all of St. Louis. This was definitely not boring. I had cleared the trip with my new boss before signing on. It wasn't quite part of the contract, but almost. He was supportive and encouraging.

Within two weeks of my walking in the door, four of ten employees had walked out, casualties of prior management conflicts and mixed loyalties. The bank's total assets shrank by close to 10 percent. What had I gotten myself into? We were trying to keep the doors open with a mere six people. The stress and tension were escalating and taking a toll. Tears and frustration were the order of the day for most, if there is a most in six. We couldn't bring in new business to offset recent losses until the staff was set. We needed people, both bodies and experience. Where would we find the right ones on which to build a future? I couldn't run a bank on temporary help for long, and I certainly couldn't go on a two-week float trip and leave my future in temporary hands. Or could I? My credibility, my son, and my big opportunity were all muddled together. The more I thought about it, the more confused I became. Ben's fall from favor seemed to provide an out, an excuse; but did it really, in the grand scheme of things that truly matter?

I chose to focus on the obvious, staffing the bank and hoping the rest would fall into place. Whether I was being naive or not, it did. First one, then a second trustworthy refugee from my old place of business signed on. Then came a couple of young nonbankers, enthusiastic, happy, ready to learn, but very green. Slowly but surely temps gave way to perms, or something like that, all in the space of a month. A semblance of stability returned. But was it enough to bet my future on? I wrestled with that question.

Ben struggled to clean up his mess, as I did mine, both of us hurtling toward a mid-May deadline. We squeezed the trip from fourteen days to twelve, part as a message to Ben that there was a price to be paid for avoidable mistakes, part as a message to my coworkers that I could sacrifice as well.

The trip was framed at its end by Memorial Day, a drop-dead date for return occasioned by Ben's finals and eighth-grade graduation, and up front by whenever we could get off. By May 9, each of Ben's teachers had reendorsed the project, subject to the performance of certain tasks and a return to certain grades, which no one at this point doubted would happen. Ben was possessed. He poured himself into reclamation, as I did into creation and organization.

Meanwhile, Patrick kept edging closer to the state track finals, finishing second in the league at Clayton and second in the regionals at Country Day the weekend before we were scheduled to depart. I was so very proud of him, of his effort and his progress. He would bid at Clayton, on May 19, for a district berth at the state championships on Memorial Day weekend. How could I miss being there for him if he made it? There is always next year—right, tell that to Patrick.

My son Bart was newly home, and I rushed him into an apartment begged off a banking client that very weekend. Betty was restive, with a slight underbelly of resentment. Patricia, at age four, was wild and crazy.

And then came a final twist—potentially cruel and clearly uncontrollable—the weather. Storm after storm powered through the Midwest that May, blowing, dumping, flooding. Cramped on one end by the school schedule, squeezed on the other by weather and work, I called each day to check on the Buffalo's water levels. There was still no flooding in northern Arkansas; the water was high but clear. Most of the moisture was tracking northeast.

I spoke to one friend who camped at Buffalo Point. He knows the river well and pronounced her high and potentially perfect *without* more rain. And still the storms lined up.

The sides were closing in. I was boxed fore and aft, high and low. We changed our departure date twice. We packed in fits and starts, between demands and doubts.

So that we wouldn't have to leave a car at our put-in spot, first my brother and then my dad planned to deliver us to Ponca. Then my brother would either meet us to float for a few days himself or pick us up when we reached the river's mouth. But where and when would we meet our neighbors from Clayton who were to join us for two days to reprovision? What would they bring? When would we start? Who would be the teller at the bank while I was gone? When would the new receptionist start? (She wouldn't; she resigned before starting, while I was on the Buffalo—I'm glad I didn't know.) And then we lost another loan—the shrink continued. My head and heart were swirling. The plan had overtaken the planner. It was the bottom of the ninth and chaos was ahead. Even my sage old dad raised the dreaded question, "Should you be doing this?"—almost, but not quite, accusing rather than asking. Believe me, I took note.

Tuesday, May 16, at 5:30 a.m., I was off to the bank for a last check. My duffel was packed; lists were strewn about—it was all there for the taking.

It hammered me as I drove the mile to work that morning amid claps of thunder: a dream, a real dream, balanced on the rim. Would it drop in, or roll harmlessly to the side? After months of planning, the agony of deciding, the moments of uncertainty, the days of rain, would we go, or would we not? More thunder and rain.

I left work at 2 p.m. Ben and I left home at 4 p.m., with a sendoff that could be called tepid at best, but was understandable nonetheless. I spent the first thirty miles explaining to Ben why Patrick, his mother, and perhaps other of his friends and their parents might feel some resentment at this appointed moment. He simply said, "I've earned it," and he had.

We ate dinner at Mom and Dad's in Springfield, purchased provisions, visited Bass Pro Shop for fishing gear, and returned in time for the woebegone weather forecast: rain, storms, tornadoes, flash flooding, all of the above.

We awoke early, planning to leave at 6:30 a.m. and drive from Springfield to Branson, where we would meet my brother and the ancient Grumman canoe on which we were betting so much, anticipating a noon launch. The first forecast said "no stupid," so we back-paddled again. We would drive down, load the canoe, return to Springfield, recheck the weather, and reach a final verdict. We shuttled, packed, fretted, fidgeted, and checked the noon outlook. Today looked grim, tomorrow a little better; but we were out of time. We would go.

And as we drove south, clouds thickened and rumbled. We passed into Arkansas; more thunder. Halfway down the long hill to Ponca,

Packed and ready to roll, with T-shirt to match.

we paused and gazed on the headwater mountains encrusted with fog. We discussed the merits of putting in at Ponca immediately— there were a few. I offered Ben a peek at the Boxley put-in upstream instead, on foot this afternoon and, with enough rise, as a full float prior to loading our gear tomorrow. The upper reaches of the Buffalo, between Boxley and Ponca, were rough, rarely floatable—I had never done it, and doing so tomorrow would put us severely behind schedule. It would also be exciting and buy time. What time? I was open to almost anything to keep the trip in play.

Ben accepted, and we headed up Boxley valley to explore. He fished and poked around. Watching Ben fish, I tried to start a journal, but it wouldn't come. It didn't until later that evening after dinner, in a cozy Ponca cabin amid the thunderclaps. Oddly enough, the first words were triggered by memories of an April 1973 Ponca launch rather than by the task at hand. I found this to be true on several occasions over the course of the next twelve days.

Heading into Ponca.

The Trip   May 17–28, 1995

Day One: May 17, 1995
Boxley and Ponca (0 miles)

What kind of blue is this in evening sky tonight?
Almost like the blue below Boxley in slanting Spring light.
Below Boxley, blue gathers clouds beneath rapids run,
languid limestone particles coalesce with morning sun . . .

—Todd Parnell, "Boxley Blue"

We were just scouting out the way upper part of the Buffalo (Boxley)
which we plan to float tomorrow. We drove most of the day, but we did
get a little fishing in and I caught the first Smallmouth of the trip. We had
a great lunch at an old fashioned smokehouse, a very historic site. It
rained mostly all day, and hopefully we'll get enough rain to float Boxley
tomorrow. I also enjoyed watching a beaver who flapped his tail at me
while I was fishing.

—Ben's journal*

The first night of our trip was spent with all the comforts of home:
hot water, hot food, dry beds. A huge mass of water and wind
descended on Missouri last night, particularly on Clayton, some 315
miles northeast, whence Betty reported downed trees. The same

* All passages from Ben's journal are unedited.

20

"Boxley Blue."

Ben at Boxley.

weather is promised for northwest Arkansas tonight with tornadoes and flash flooding. We're staying put. I've already been there in April 1973.

Why this excuse for chickening out today after all the planning, the highs and lows, the steps forward and back, the ins and outs? Spring, and my memories of Mother Buffalo twenty-two years ago last month. Tomorrow we will float, come hell or high water, or any combination thereof.

I shared the story of that April past with Ben tonight in hopes of easing his disappointment at losing yet another night on the river. It was the first time I had touched on the details of that earlier washout with him. The reminiscence was painful in some ways. I recall that there was at least one drowning, if not more, on the Buffalo as a result of that storm.

We hope to launch tomorrow at Boxley, six boulder-strewn heavy-drop miles above the normal Ponca put-in. We drove up Boxley valley earlier today. The water was high and will be challenging if we get enough rain tonight. Enough rain—the floater's dilemma. What is enough rain? What is too much, particularly when the creek is full? From the sounds outside, anything is possible.

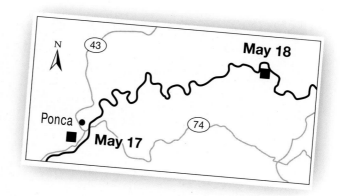

Day Two: May 18, 1995
Ponca to below Erbie Ford (16 miles)

Autumn and Spring are her mornings of glory,
when the rain from the mountains puts blood in her veins.
If you listen quite clearly she will tell you a story
of a course now forgotten, and the one that remains.

   —Dr. W. P. Parnell, "Swan Creek Song"

Very rough day, full of dangerous rapids with a canoe with too much gear to handle. A cold front came through and it got down to 40 degrees tonight. We didn't have much fishing time, too much paddling, 16 miles. While I was getting firewood, a cottonmouth slid across my arm, but for some reason, probably the cold, it didn't bite me. After that my dad and I managed to get ten hours of sleep.

   —Ben's journal

    Well, today it happened. The dream became real. For Ben, the culmination of nearly two years of effort and focus. For me, who knows? A quest? For what, I'm not sure. A return visit to my youth, a midlife crisis, a fantasy camp? Those answers are all too simple. Maybe I'll know at journey's end.

Prepared for launch at Ponca.

Ben and Roark Bluff.

As usual, the day didn't go as planned. As I sit here this evening, somewhat beaten and battered, a bit frightened and overwhelmed, and definitely old, I marvel at the folly of planning nature's course.

It had rained all night, surely enough for us to do Boxley. "Needed five inches' rise; only got three," they said—they being the folks at Lost Valley Canoe Rental who would have put us in, and their determination carried authority, given our need to rent from them for a Boxley run. They are nice folks and looked after our car while we were out. They shared our sense of excitement about the journey ahead.

So, we were off to the Ponca Bridge put-in to begin. Disappointment at not being able to float from Boxley gave way to anticipation. The water was up and beautiful.

The canoe loading was eventful only in that we got everything in. Following a ceremonial photograph by a chuckling stranger, we were off. We walked the first shoal to get a sense of the canoe's balance. It was perfect, but we had no buoyancy. This was a problem—not unexpected, but a problem nonetheless.

The upper Buffalo, with its high clear water and rushing, rowdy rapids, offers perfect spring floating. Here we are with limited maneuverability and no room for misjudgment. All we can do is set the course, hoping it's the right one and that the haystacks don't get us or we don't end up sideways in the current. Haystacks, for the uninitiated, are points of concentration in a rapid where water flows surge together to create large whitecaps capable of dumping cold water in the bow-person's lap. I've seen haystacks sink a canoe. Generally it's a rather harmless and humorous sight. Not today, please.

Stunning bluffs guard the entrance to each chute: Bee Bluff; Roark Bluff, with black facing; Big Bluff, some five hundred feet from top to bottom, among the tallest between the Appalachians and the Rockies; Jim Bluff, with ancient mineral teardrops. We encounter a new one at each bend. This stretch of stream defies the term *average* and exceeds even the grandest of expectations, time after time after time.

The day grew windy and cooler, with skating clouds, as the cold front that had flushed out the rains pushed through the upper Buffalo watershed. We became wetter with each rapid.

For once, the seriousness of what had always seemed daring and fun overtook me. In our canoe lay our means of making it for ten or eleven more days: dry duffel, iced-down food and drink. Ahead lay a

Approaching Big Bluff.

Jim Bluff with its "mineral teardrops."

forty-degree night. If we flipped, we could lose the canoe and all the rest. If we were fortunate enough to salvage the contents and the vehicle, there would be little time to dry out. Alone, with wet gear, in cold weather, and with no place to go but downriver—the possibility was not a frivolous one. Perhaps I sensed a tiny piece of the rush our forefathers felt when they left home to travel west. There was no margin of error for them, little for us. But then again, we have ice, waterproof matches, and a Therm-a-Rest, that marvelous sleeping pad that smooths rocks and keeps old tired backs like mine from locking up—so, forget melodramatic analogies. But I still have to keep the Thermorest dry, don't I?

After a chilly lunch below Hemmed-in Hollow, we were back in the canoe ready for the larger tasks ahead. Hemmed-in Hollow is worth visiting for itself. A half mile up a horseshoe canyon, it is the highest waterfall in the midlands, another wonder tucked into this small corner of northwest Arkansas. Depending on rain and season, water pours or trickles over a smooth lip straight to the crystal pool below, some two hundred feet. A midsummer's shower in the spray is bracing and unforgettable. This time we passed.

Farther down on the left lies an unnamed, but unmatched, feeder spring. Its waters, never ceasing, stairstep down ancient rock ledges, entering the Buffalo with barely a ripple, adding a bright blue-green flow of mountain runoff. I walked up its steps once, but they extended much farther than I had time to travel. Time. One could invest so much of it here.

We heard the Rock Garden long before we found it: forty to fifty yards of pounding whitecaps and slippery rocks with sudden dips and drops and an ever-changing course, depending on water conditions. It would be too difficult to walk, we reasoned, and entered left center. We should have gone right center.

Halfway through I jumped out, as did Ben. We held the canoe against the torrent, trying to assess our position. We were stuck in the middle and desperate for an escape route. We chose to try and nurse the canoe cross-current to the left bank. We should have tried right. We made the bank and slid into a downed tree. We pushed and pulled but were unable to dislodge. Ben asked for the hatchet, the first good idea of the run, though from the look in his eyes I was unsure if he intended to use it on me or on the tree. He began chopping at the claw

Above Gray Rock Shoals.

holding us captive and, after fifteen long minutes, broke through it. We walked the canoe on down the bank and breathed a sigh of relief, only to anticipate Gray Rock.

But yet another surprise waited before the Rock: a swift, narrow channel with several feet of drop over a distance of twenty yards. We had no choice but to slide into the "V" and hang on. We bounced through, taking on water from frothy haystacks, but stuck on the ledge at the bottom. The canoe swung sideways into the rapid. We wobbled wildly and dipped toward the current, me screaming "balance, balance, balance!" and Ben doing just that. The current shook us free before it sank us, and we drifted clear. This was pure good fortune—nothing more, nothing less. I honestly had thought we were gone.

Then we heard the roar of the Rock. The only way to take the rapid was by foot. Weary and wary, we inched into the fury, on the right side, as far from the looming downstream shadow as possible. We pushed and pulled, slipped and fell, and struggled through the one hundred yards of chaos. It would have been great fun with an empty canoe and with dry gear awaiting us, but the experience was nothing but sinister today. When we reached the end, we reentered the current and simply drifted by the shoal's menacing namesake. After all that, we still had to pass within five feet of it. We did, and it was gone, more a visual than an actual threat.

And then came Kyles Landing, the traditional takeout point for an upper Buffalo float. It was cold and late in the afternoon, and we still had miles to go. At least the next stretch would be easier. Ahead, I thought, were no more compressed chutes of cold water that we could neither run nor walk. No more standing waves to slap our cold bodies. No more risk to our "drydom." Wrong.

Shortly after Kyles, we entered a narrow shoot with nothing but wave after wave of cold fury that wasn't supposed to be there. We tried to walk her to the right. The current was focused and controlling, even to the step. Ben fell first, righting himself, then smashing his hand between the canoe and rocks. I shouted for him to slow down. He tried, but he couldn't, shaking his hand in pain. I hung on to the back of the canoe, slipping, but desperate to retain a grip on our livelihood for the next ten days, particularly tonight. We slid through, then I went. My ankle banged against a boulder, then my foot. As we pushed on, I had no feeling in the toe whose nail I would soon shed. Clear of the current, we reentered the canoe, now confused, tired, hurting, and worried about our gear and ourselves; and this was only the first day on the river.*

It was cold and windy and soon to rain when we found a gravel bar high enough to set up camp. We hurried to beat the clouds; as I raised the tent, Ben sought wood to warm us. I heard a cry, and he was back. As Ben had grabbed a pile of small sticks, a small water

---

* Fearing that "some city slicker" might imitate me, a reader questioned whether I should "give away my ineptness" in "walking a canoe through rapids." I generally agree that exiting a canoe midrapids is amateurish at best, and I will always encourage anyone I'm with to stay put. At the same time, textbook theory didn't provide much comfort with an overladen canoe and standing waves sufficient to sink it. Given similar circumstances, I'd probably act "inept" again.

Our first campsite in the welcome early morning sun.

moccasin had crawled out and over his hand, not biting, perhaps because of the cold. Not striking—thank God. What is this water moccasin? *Agkistrodon piscivorus* is also called cottonmouth because of the white throat it displays as it threatens to bury its fangs in flesh. *Piscivorus* means "fish eating," if that is any comfort. Whether a cottonmouth bite would have proved a trip-ender would have depended on a lot of things, including dosage and when the snake had last struck.

We went to bed after sixteen miles that first day at a little after 8:00 p.m. I don't remember what we ate. We awoke at 7:00 a.m. the next morning. I hadn't slept eleven hours straight for years. It's a habit that would grow on me over the next two weeks.

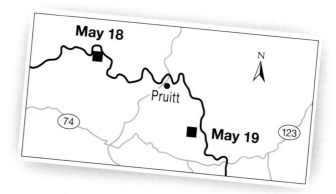

Day Three: May 19, 1995
Erbie to the Little Buffalo (12 miles)

There's a beauty in the river,
there's a beauty in the stream

    —Ozark Mountain Daredevils, "Beauty in the River"

I managed to catch about 40 fish today, and a couple of nice ones. Today
was a lot easier than yesterday, and we fished a lot more too. We met the
Huffords at Pruitt and they're going to be with us for the rest of the weekend. Today was a lot warmer and a pretty, not cloudy day. I tested pH
levels out of the Little Buffalo and the main Buffalo; the pH came out the
same. I will test further down and see what happens. I have also taken
samples at Boxley and Pruitt.

    —Ben's journal

    Today, Friday, dawned cool and wet, but soon the sun appeared and
all was well. The sleep, the unexpected challenges, and the cold gave
way to a new day of bugless gravel bar and hot coffee. Cold nights
work miracles when warmed by sunlight.
    The first rapid stabbed home our vulnerability as we started in,
backed out, and paid homage to its compressed fury. We walked but
didn't fall or slip. Fear gave way to smiles as each successive shoal

Floatin' down the river.

proved kinder and gentler, and the sun shone brighter and warmer. We fished, we laughed, we thought of the trip ahead with anticipation and a new sense of reality. It was no longer a game, if indeed it ever had been.

Erbie to Pruitt seemed nondescript, plain. Along this stretch there are no significant landmarks or memorable sights. It is not mentioned on the map or in the guidebooks. Why? It is surely beautiful compared to most stretches of river. But after Ponca's top ten miles, it doesn't stand up, through no fault of its own.

We met our Clayton neighbors, Duff Hufford and his son Dan, right at the appointed hour, and were greeted with a welcome touch of home. We had been gone only three days, and out for only two, but fresh food and company were as nice as the warm, dry weather. We fished, floated, and napped in the company of no one other than ourselves.

Napping on a gravel bar is considered a complex undertaking by some. How does one sleep on rocks? The answer is really quite simple. Find a spot under a tree for shade and proceed as follows: first,

A river nap.

remove all stones greater than the size of one's hand from the napping site; second, place your life jacket or a similar cushioned device at the top of the site for a pillow; third, lay your weary carcass down on the gravel and wiggle slightly until the site conforms to your body size and type; fourth, pull the bill of your cap or hat over your eyes; fifth, listen to the music of birds backed by rippling water—then sleep. River naps generally last less than an hour but reenergize body and soul for crawling back into a canoe to face the fish and rapids that lie ahead. The one downside to a river nap is having to rise from a prone position without benefit of anything or anyone to hang on to, while slightly buzzed from sound sleep. Brief renaps are permitted if one falls flat into the original nap site. Fortunately, even the old guys arose uneventfully this late afternoon.

We finished one beautiful day on the river with huge steaks and a perfect campsite at the mouth of the Little Buffalo.

Ben fly-fishing the Little Buffalo before dinner.

As Ben assembled his fly rod and stalked confidently up the Baby Buff, I felt awe in the timelessness of it all. Some 150 years ago, his grandfather to the sixth or seventh power, Abner Casey, is said to have walked as tall at Parthenon, Arkansas, a few miles up the Little Buffalo, where he was supposedly buried in the 1850s.

Why Ben, why here, why now? Who knows. "Eventually, all things merge into one, and a river runs through it. . . . On some of these rocks are timeless raindrops. Under the rocks are the words, and some of the words are theirs." Norman Maclean said it all.

Good night Abner. Good night Ben. Good night river.

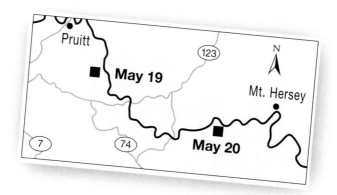

Day Four: May 20, 1995
Little Buffalo past Hasty (10 miles)

We are part of the great passion. I am of this place.

　—Harry Middleton, *The Earth Is Enough*

No entry.

　—Ben's journal

Another day in Eden. Perfect temperature, perfect weather, perfect sky. The fears from the Ponca stretch have ebbed. Perhaps they will surface again, but not today. The Huffords are going to be spoiled.

Today we floated—actually floated—with a bountiful current to carry us. No aching arms or sore backsides tomorrow. Nature's beauty was yet again of a different kind, but ever present. We saw waterfalls originating at the tops of bluffs, animals of every sort and type, and fish—many, many fish. Big ones, small ones, dark ones, light ones: the stream is alive and teeming with energy. The day is exquisite, and we are one with it.

We stopped for lunch, then again napped in the shade, the ever present sound of running water soothing city strains. We floated on past the Hasty low-water bridge, portaging rather than running, and beneath Highway 123. We found a magnificent campsite, high on a

Morning cleanup.

Settling into river life.

A room with a view.

gravel spit with running water, a small bluff to front it, and a large one ahead—"a room with a view" we decided.

We found camaraderie as well. The river is about independence, isolation, and self-direction; but it is a natural soup pot as well, drawing in all who visit and blending their diversity into a warm, comforting broth of brotherhood. I'm obviously writing this over a glass of wine.

In actual fact, I've never had a fight on the river; well, almost never. There was that last evening of a family adventure on the lower Buffalo some seven or eight years ago. Betty and I had decided late one July to take a family float, to allow Patrick and Ben (this was pre-Patricia) a chance to commune with Mother Buffalo. This was to be our sons' introduction to the mother lode of nature's blessings. We did it in July so it wouldn't be dangerous, just exciting. Ben was six, Patrick nine, and Betty and I old enough to know better.

Each day was beautiful, dry, and touching; each evening, calm and cool. We ate veal piccata the first night, chicken breasts and fresh asparagus the next, everything on plan and on schedule.

At midafternoon on day three we stopped at a special spot, where three branches of low green river ran their individual gentle courses.

We unloaded the canoes and allowed the boys to run the rapid on their own, and on film no less. They were proud, but becoming all too perturbed at their father's video camera. We lingered for hours at this private perfect place, the cool summer wind picking up, white clouds racing atop the facing bluff.

Miles away a weather front was gathering steam. Unbeknownst to us, it was loaded with wind and water and would soon take aim on the Parnell family campsite, an experience that might not have been all that bad if we had camped where we were supposed to.

Reluctantly, we loaded up and left our Eden (there's that word again), Betty and Patrick anxious to be on, Ben and I lingering as usual. I asked them to stop at Elephant's Head Rock a few miles downstream. There were several nice gravel bars thereabouts, and we would have a simple five-mile paddle the following day. They nodded and set sail.

An hour later, as Ben and I pulled into view of the big Elephant's Head profile, Betty and Patrick were nowhere to be found. I wondered aloud if they had missed it, but even six-year-old Ben looking at the rock said, "No way." After all, if you've ever seen an elephant in the zoo, on the screen, or in the wild, and Betty had all three, there was no mistaking the remarkable likeness of nature's cut on this bluff: thick, prominent trunk, sunken eyes—eerie to stare into.

We paddled on, past the last two decent gravel bars toward the White River. Still no canoe. One never camps near the White. The rise and fall of water from the dam upstream as late summer air-conditioners pull power from electric company generators results in water-level variations at the mouth of the Buffalo of up to ten feet. This constant ebb and flow in late summer also renders the big bars at Buffalo's end full of weeds, bugs, and muck—not the perfect campsites to which we had become accustomed.

I began to stew and steam. It was becoming apparent that Elephant or no, the lead canoe was barreling toward trip's end oblivious to the consequences. The sky was also taking on an ominous tint, moving from the blues and greens of midday to yellow and gray. Winds were beginning to gust; in the distance, thunder clapped.

As we reached the last bend of the Buffalo, a johnboat trailing a canoe appeared, headed back toward us. Betty and Patrick sat defiantly as Ben screamed above the motor, "Dad's really *xxxxed*," or

Elephant Head Rock.

something like that. The johnboat's pilot, who also, ironically, was named Parnell, and I'm not making this up, agreed to tow us all back upstream to the first inhabitable gravel bar. I was speechless.

As we sat linked together by rope, I asked how this could have happened. "There was no Elephant," was the reply. "Didn't you see the trunk, the eyes?" "There were no ears," I was told. *NO EARS*? Were they supposed to flap in the wind? What about a tail?

I stormed ashore, barking orders to erect tents as the first wave of storms hit. We got one up and began to work on the next. Wind roared through the valley, lifted our first tent skyward, then rolled it like a ball along the gravel. I'll never forget Ben chasing it, giggling giddily.

The tent simply blew away. One moment it was up; the next it was gone. We never saw it again. We threw up the second one between gusts and staked it soundly. It held as the furor subsided.

We tried to eat the huge steak saved for our final night's feast. Between storms, in the dark, the charcoal finally caught and we nursed the heat. We cut strips of sirloin straight from the grill and stuffed them in our mouths, blood rare and barely room temperature in the middle. That was dinner—steak and steak. In fact, it was awfully good. Even my humor brightened as we four crawled into our two-man tent, not quite but almost stacked atop each other.

At midnight, another round of storms arrived. One collapsed the tent upon us as tether ropes were jerked from the gravel by grappling gusts. I stood outside and held up the tent during one period of particular fury. Then, back inside, I found water puddled and the sheets soaked. I cursed, Betty huddled, Patrick groused, and Ben slept—slept through the whole thing.

As we crawled from our trashed tent into the morning sunlight, we managed a hug, a smile—and Ben slept. All of which has been a roundabout way of saying that, though rare, anger toward one another on the river does occur, usually to dissipate with the first rays of the sun.

As Duff, Dan, Ben, and I sat around the campfire that night in May 1995, sharing stories and laughter, I reveled in the companionship. I also realized how far we had to go if we were to meet our next and last appointed rendezvous, with my brother at Rush five days hence. We would have to cover sixty-five miles from Sunday morning to Friday noon. I reasoned that we would reach the Narrows on Sunday,

From left: Todd, Ben, Duff, and Dan.

Red Bluff on Monday, past Gilbert on Tuesday, Maumee on Wednesday, beyond Buffalo Point on Thursday, and Rush at midday on Friday. As usual, I would be off, way off.

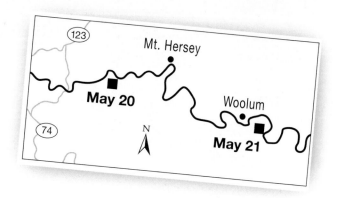

Day Five: May 21, 1995
Past Hasty to Point Peter Mountain (15 miles)

I will drink from the river,
that runs down from the mountain.
Just my life returning.

—Ozark Mountain Daredevils, "Colorado Song"

The fishing was horrible today. I only caught about ten fish all day. Four
of them were bass. The Huffords have left, and me and my dad are alone
again. A squirrel fell in the water right next to our boat. We went through
the ugliest stretch of the river I have ever seen at Woolum, and the water
is extremely murky. I took a pH test at Woolum and it came out the same?

—Ben's journal

We arose to light rain and coolness. Duff and Dan packed for home:
wet clothes in this cooler, dirty things in that box, extra food to our
coolers. We can't afford the weight of wet clothes or extra boxes, so
we will wear the dirty clothes. It is a different perspective. We must
keep our eye on the end, the goal, and how to best get there, rather
than what is easy or expedient.

Saying good-bye to the Huffords at Mt. Hersey.

We begin a long stretch alone now. Duff and Dan will be with us to Mt. Hersey, then return to Clayton. We have much time to make up and much distance to cover, sixty miles in four and a half days, which to us itinerant floaters is no mean task.

As we parted at midday, the independence and interdependence of our lot, that of Ben and me, over the next week became ever clearer. For Ben, the exuberance of not having to go "home" as usual was the dominating mood. It revealed itself in a calmness. In the Huffords I saw a sense of loss at leaving, of wanting, I think, to stay and carry on. For me, the focus was again on how to assure our safety and soundness (I've not yet escaped banking), our dryness, our progress, out here, on our own. I have never seen Ben so elated or animated. I have probably never worried more about less.

The river is changing character and color. We float longer and flatter stretches. Except for the occasional slate rapid channeling the current to large whitecaps, the rapids are largely steerable, with no need for strong strokes or side movement.

The calming water.

Ahead looms John Redell Bluff. I read from the map to Ben, "perfectly symmetrical." He asked what that meant. I tried to explain. He shook his head. I asked what it looked like to him. "The same on both sides," he said. He clearly understood the new word.

And it's still cool, maybe even cold. In any event, we were chilled. So we did what any self-respecting river rat would do. We found a beautiful, small gravel bar high along a swift rapid and built a huge fire. We made no pretense at starting this one with twigs, leaves, and dried moss. We piled on limbs and logs, then doused them heavily with charcoal lighter. The resultant rip-roaring blaze made our rain gear hot to the touch and warmed our bodies and souls in less than fifteen minutes. We shared a quiet lunch and stared into the whitecaps from our perch. Even with no sun to glint the water, it sparkled, alive. Under the dark gray sky, it bounced and banged in a chorus of subtle colors and clatter, rushing by with power and grace. I sat and watched and felt the cleansing nature of it all. Mundane burdens gave way to soothing sounds and gray glitter. I began to melt that day on the gravel bar. The cold hardness of daily grind and city clutter slipped downstream and left me calm and sedentary. The thaw would go on for days.

I looked at Ben and wondered what he was feeling. I didn't ask because he, too, was enmeshed in tranquil undertones.

Sometime later, without word or cue, we rose, repacked, and moved on. A defining moment of the journey had passed. Soon the sun shone on us as well.

We carried on at a faster pace, aware of time, paddling slow stretches, casting our lines into fast water. The map warned of a small waterfall, which at low water was worrisome. With our baggage, it would probably be trouble at any water level. We heard it first, then saw it: a clean, straight cut across the water, with maybe a slight V on the left. We pulled over to the left bank to scout and walked fifty feet to the dropoff. Farther down on the left, a young man and woman had strewed gear across the gravel to dry. They had obviously guessed wrong.

We found a slot and debated the merits of walking versus running. Ben won out. I wasn't wild about getting wet, but we were lighter after four days, and the warm sun was out. We would go for it. The dropoff appeared to be eighteen to twenty-four inches, with a clear chute if we hit it correctly and no apparent ledge to hang us up at the bottom.

As we approached the roar, I felt not fear but focus. As we slipped through the appointed aperture and settled safely in white foam beneath, waves lapping at our laps, I felt exhilaration. Ben uttered a guttural exclamatory, our first cry of victory. We were through, racing past our sodden comrades on the bank. This was fun—for us, not them. They waved nonetheless, partners in the pursuit.

And then we approached a part of the river I had not seen since I was sixteen, one that contains several notable Buffalo landmarks, one of which displays the power and majesty of the river past.

To the south (our right) and yet unseen, Richland Creek pours in, maybe a mile ahead. Eons ago, it had flowed in here at the Narrows, a long, low finger of rock that once marked the confluence of the Richland and the Buffalo. I believe Richland Creek is the Buffalo's third largest tributary. The Little Buffalo of Abner Casey ranks first or second. I know from conversations with others that upper Richland Creek boasts some of the most remote and extraordinary scenery in North America. Another time, another trip.

The Narrows stretches maybe one hundred feet, perhaps two hundred, above the river, a long narrow spit of rock, dipping, barren in the middle and raised at both ends. It is climbable and represents yet another classic Buffalo River photo op, but we have "miles to go before we sleep." Another time, another trip. I've said that twice in the past fifteen lines. I said it endlessly on the river. The Buffalo River watershed offers so much to see, to do, to explore, to experience—it could take a lifetime.

We rounded a bend to greet a cave high on an orange bluff fronting us. As I pulled over to the left for a picture, a fisherman motoring upstream said, "Wait for the next one." He was right.

I want to go back to this spot soon, for it intrigued me. It was the first time I had been on this stretch of the river since my youth. I needed more time with it.

I took more pictures here than elsewhere, but, as luck would have it, after our return to St. Louis this was the roll of thirty-six exposures that the film processor lost, this one roll out of the ten I took. The clerk at "my Schnucks Market" had the nerve to say that they would kindly replace it with a free roll. Replace? Re-create a piece of this voyage, of my lost youth? What could that insensitive idiot be thinking? Photographs are limited in their capacity to capture, but they do provide a reference point. I'll become fuzzy about these scenes and this part of the trip without them, free roll of film notwithstanding. All of which is to say, I must return (I doubt Ben will object), retake, and use a different film processor.

Woolum Ford was crowded and ugly. A large fishing party had gathered and was setting up camp on the left, across from the modern-day Richland Creek merger with Mother Buffalo. Trucks, gear, coolers, and tarps were strewn across the large flat gravel bar. Fishermen filtered in, soon twenty or more of them, to eat, drink, and story themselves into oblivion. It brought back more memories.

I'd been on several of these "catered" floats with the dean of float guides, Mr. Burl Cox, and family or fishing buddies. They are everything that they are advertised to be—all, at least most, of the comforts of home; being waited on hand and foot; fantastically fattening, gorgeously greasy food; sheets and pillows on your cot. You raise nary a finger for a day or two, except to move your bulging carcass from one camp chair to another, from johnboat to campfire. You consume large quantities of saturated fat and drink daunting doses of Budweiser. If you're with Burl, you hear wild tales of days gone past—perhaps a grain of truth, but no more, in each. You go home constipated and with a hangover, unless you usually eat and drink like this.

One morning of one trip stands tall in my memory. It's a tale told over and over among my friends. Most who hear are either unable to relate or simply don't believe. It was a unique morning.

The day started with a headache, hot sun, and no fish. I was in a johnboat with my brother; Ralph Kalish, a longtime friend and partner in political debate who once worked for Richard Nixon as a misguided youth, managing the eastern Missouri machine for CREEP, the Committee to Re-elect the President; and guide Burl. Ralph didn't fish much, didn't get out of the city very often, and was thoroughly enjoying himself, perched midships reading Mark Twain, as I recall. My brother and I were dutifully, if languidly, flailing the waters with an ever changing assortment of lures.

This was the last day of an uneventful trip, and Burl decided to liven things up a bit. First, it was a frog, a very large bullfrog. "Boys, you see that frog over yonder?" (He always started his sentences with "Boys.") We didn't, and I'm not sure we ever would have had Burl not slipped us silently under a branch, brought forth a small piece of cane with a hook and piece of red yarn attached to it, dangled it in front of the frog's nose, and then begun to walk it along the frog's body, seeking a nook or cranny in which to sink the hook. The frog, incidentally, just sat there looking dumb. With a swift and sudden jerk that snapped us all to attention, Burl gaffed the critter and lifted its flailing body into the canoe, where he swiftly dispatched it to the live box. "Boys—lunch," he muttered.

But then he thought of the six other happy, hungry campers needing to be fed, and how many frogs that would take. "Boys, I'm gonna show you something my granddaddy showed me when I was a boy, and maybe get us a little more lunch at the same time, but you can't tell a soul." OK, we nodded (sorry, Burl), and sat quietly as he began to scan the rocky bank to the left.

A few moments later, as we were joined by a second johnboat, Burl pulled us over to a long stretch of rock shelf, about waist deep, with running water. He stationed veteran law-abiding citizen Don Deters upstream as a lookout and less exacting Bill Wenthe downstream. "Boys, if you see anyone a'comin', you tell me real fast 'cause I don't want to go to jail." He then stripped off every last shred of clothing and slipped into the water along the ledge. Ralph looked at me with saucer eyes and questions he was afraid to raise. I could only shrug. Burl sat there, moving occasionally, for three to four minutes, concentrating fiercely, as if in a trance, hands moving beneath and around the rock. Then, with a broad grin, the trance was broken, except perhaps for Ralph, who continued to stare in disbelief, not sure he wanted to be witnessing whatever it was that was going down. Burl's grin said it all, and then the statement of fact, "Boys, there's two of them big ones in there, twelve to fourteen pounds apiece. You reckon we ought to get us some lunch?"

What we were witnessing, as accessories to the crime, was the ancient art of "noodlin'," or grabbing large fish, normally catfish, with your hands. Someone will occasionally grab a snapping turtle, snake, or particularly large catfish that will leave a lasting memory with the perpetrator, which is why Burl only explores with his hands these days and doesn't wrestle them out mano a mano. Regardless, his act

Burl Cox with an appetizer.

Burl feelin' for big cats.

of daring is highly illegal and deemed unfair to fish. I'm not sure why. I'm only sure that I will never try it.

Burl unstrung his short cane and spent the next thirty minutes maneuvering it beneath the ledge, attaching the cord to the mouth of the large whiskered catfish swimming beneath. I'm still not sure how he did it all. I know only that it was a delicate and risky undertaking.

At last he smiled again and called to Ralph, who still had not moved or uttered his first word, which for Ralph was no small accomplishment. Ralph hesitantly waded to Burl's side and with genuine trepidation accepted the empty end of the rope. I cocked my camera. "Boy, why don't you just go and lift her up," said Burl smiling slightly. As he did so, the water exploded with fifteen pounds of raging, thrashing fury, slapping Ralph's legs and draining the blood from his face. Burl laughed and laughed, as did we all. Ralph asked Burl why he had to take all his clothes off. We all laughed more. Burl never answered that one.

He tied the cat up and went back for more. Another fifteen to twenty minutes passed before he waved for another city slicker. Since I was the staff photographer, my brother wrestled this one, about the same size.

Ralph Kalish earns an assist.

The catfish man.

After the show, the cast posed for pictures. Left to right: Don Deters, Bill Wenthe, Ralph Kalish, Pat and Todd Parnell, Barry Bell; kneeling in front: Burl Cox and Tom Schaefer.

Burl was flushed and elated. He quickly dressed and reached into his tackle box. He pulled out a pint of Evan Williams bourbon in a plain brown paper sack and took a long draw. He passed the sack, and we could tell that it was not proper river etiquette to turn him down, even at 10:15 a.m. The bourbon was soon gone, and we were floating again, with two noodled flathead catfish, a set of frog legs, and an enormous buzz in tow.

Suddenly the comic potential struck us, or maybe it was the Evan Williams. The elaborate plan we hatched was strictly spontaneous and clearly bourbon based. As the younger set of our entourage, namely Barry Bell and Tom Schaefer, pulled round the bend, they were greeted with a bit of Buffalo drama.

Picture this if you can: City slicker Ralph is draped back in his chair reading, with Burl's small cane pole dangling in the water. Suddenly, the river erupts in furious fashion. Water splashing, line pulling, Ralph sits stunned, trying desperately to hang on to the small cane pole. Finally, it is simply too much; he is pulled in, headfirst. I am waving a huge fishing net at the madness; as Ralph disappears into the depths, I dive after him, net in hand. We both surface shortly, me with a huge catfish in the net, Ralph sputtering and cursing.

The group had gathered. Our friends were aghast, pulling aside and ready to join in the rescue. Then Burl could hold back no more. Tears rolled from his eyes as his stifled laughter spilled across the water. When my brother joined him, the others recognized this scurrilous pantomime and began to howl as well. Maybe you had to be there.

This was high drama on the Buffalo, starring Burl's catfish, securely tied to the cane pole, avowed nonangler Ralph, and a few innocent bystanders. Another pint of Evan Williams appeared. Fried catfish was never better. This was a long-winded way of saying there is a place for catered floats, but not today, not for Ben and me at least.

As we passed the fishing camp, Richland Creek joined on the right, looking innocent and flat. Farther up its banks are magnificent waterfalls, canoe-bashing rocks, and sparkling springs. As before, another trip.

A new freshwater scourge had now joined us—cows. Cows are great to eat, rare, grilled, dripping red juice. They are terrible river partners. They foul the water if granted free stream-wallowing rights and soil the perfect gravel bar. We wondered aloud, why cows on a

National River? Apparitions? Political favors from President Bill? I've yet to find out, but for a stretch of a mile or two there were cows, the only such place along the way.

In fact, the water below Richland Creek turned ugly and murky, the gravel bars flattened, and the terrain bordered on boring. For the first time in five days, the Buffalo became ordinary. We paddled on, hoping to escape the mundane, muddy mess and wondering at the cause of this sudden shift to silt and pasture.

Dusk settled, and again for the first time in five days, no gravel bar beckoned, no sheltering bluffs cast shadows, no river "bathtub" surfaced. We began to worry about a campsite. We finally chose a spot that was high enough but backed up to a field with a few stale bovine dumplings decorating the rocks. The water ran greenish brown past several large rocks on the far bank, and we looked due south to Point Peter Mountain. We wondered if rain farther up Richland Creek could have contributed to the condition of the water. Tomorrow would tell.

The evening was warm and dry, a change for the better. As Ben worked math problems, chicken grilled and the sun set. I was comforted by the solitude of it all.

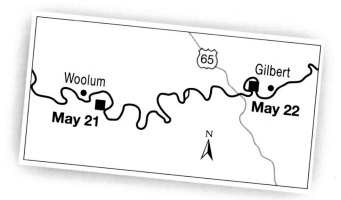

Day Six: May 22, 1995
Point Peter Mountain past the Highway 65 Bridge (15 miles)

People who return from long, quiet fishing trips . . . are a little defensive about having put so much time to "no account" because there's no intellectual justification for what they've been doing. But the returned fisherman usually has a peculiar abundance of gumption, usually for the very same things he was sick to death of a few weeks before. He hasn't been wasting time. It's only our limited cultural viewpoint that makes it seem so.

—Robert M. Pirsig, *Zen and the Art of Motorcycle Maintenance*

Today was a much prettier day, partly because of the weather and because of the beautiful scenery. We traveled 15 miles and I saw a turkey fly across the river. We did fish a little bit and caught a couple of really nice fish, one that almost weighed three pounds. There are turtles stacked up about every five feet along the river, and I've never seen so many in my life. I think they're laying eggs up on the shore. We didn't do any water testing at all.

—Ben's journal

Day six emerged from a blanket of fog and dew, more like the good old summer floating to which we are accustomed. The campsite proved prettier than it had seemed last evening. The water had cleared to green from brown, its murkiness still a mystery. The vista to Point Peter was clear and clean, and the air was warm. We finally used our radio to check the forecast. A chance of thunderstorms; we need to camp high again tonight.

The sun was hot and the water ever more blue. Bluffs and rocks reentered the landscape, and we determined that the two-mile float from Woolum to our previous night's campsite was an aberration.

A large Smallmouth cracked the morning calm. In typical brownie style, it attacked rather than bit the quarter-ounce jig and pig at the end of my line. It vibrated in my hands, pounding at the pole with a fury matched only by the pounding in my chest. Those who have been there know that the thrill is unparalleled: a large brownie in fast water darting under rocks, seeking shelter, occasionally leaping, and finally diving under the canoe, back and forth, up and down, never giving in until the end. In fifteen minutes we had worked our way over to the side of the current, and I was able to reach down and thumb the quivering mouth. The fish weighed two and three quarters or maybe three pounds—not a lunker, but a challenge most worthy. When I think of fishing, I think of the Smallmouth, with its bronze sides and

A gentle rapid.

angry red eyes, mean, strong, confident in its surroundings, the ultimate warrior. After I took a picture or two (among those lost), he or she was back in the current, slipping slowly into deeper water. We would both sleep well tonight. More important, Ben would soon latch onto one of similar size, his first of such magnitude. And he would never again be the same.

Here I've been complaining about last night's gravel bar, and now it doesn't seem so bad. What's the deal? Catching a large Smallmouth smoothes all. But as I mull it over, it is a weighty subject—gravel bar selection, that is.

To some, selection of the evening accommodation borders on the religious: the Holy Grail of Gravel, the Yin and Yang of gentle nights. The Ten Commandments of Camping on the River, as handed down to me by River Lords of fact and fable, are:

  I. HIGH CAMPSITES—safe from flooding
  II. SMALL GRAVEL—easy sleeping
  III. RUNNING WATER—river baths
  IV. BIG BLUFFS—good aesthetics
  V. NO STANDING WATER—no mosquitos
  VI. PILES OF FIREWOOD—tall tales around the campfire
  VII. NO ISLANDS—in case you need an escape route
  VIII. NO ONE ELSE—a sacred law that may be breached only in dire emergency
  IX. WESTERN EXPOSURE—so you can see to eat dinner, and sleep in the next morning
  X. NO COWS

There you have it, straight from the top. In the final analysis, what really matters are elevation, gravel, running water, and big bluffs, and I've been known to settle for three out of four.

The Buffalo makes site selection simple. It is remote and uncrowded, the water almost always runs, and most gravel bars are elevated and face rock. After years of camping on the river, with each site more magnificent than the one before, I can bear witness. And over time, with minor variation, the classics remain, untouched, unchanged. There's one favorite, on the right side of the river just after the put-in at Ponca, that says it all. Elevated, small, exclusive, sheltered by bluffs and trees, with deep running water at the base of a rapid, the site always temps me to pull over, no matter the hour. In fact, there are many such sites; this one just happens to hold a romantic memory or two for Betty and me.

Site selection usually begins about 5:00 p.m. It's deemed OK to grab the perfect gravel bar prior to then. It's not socially acceptable to settle for less until after 7:00 p.m. This two-hour window of decision can be a source of tension, in that perfect is unarguably in the eye of the beholder. I tend to hold out. Betty, on the other hand, is easy and soon anxious; yin and yang again.

On this trip, Ben and I had few moments of campsite anxiety. The stretch after Woolum yesterday afternoon was one. In the end, we settled for less, which became more as we settled in. Enough about gravel already.

Nature stirred around Ben and me. Buzzards circled; turtles lined up in perfect formation, sometimes twenty to a log; a graceful blue heron settled into its nest amid a colony of others. A turkey flew across the river ahead. Ben took aim with his paddle and dropped the luckless bird in his mind. As it flew on, he gazed at its splendor.

And then a C-17 or B-52 or B-1, a *BIG* bomber, flew over at hilltop level, shattering the silence, killing chirps, murdering the music of the river. Ben thought it was crashing. I assured him it was practicing, playing with our tax dollars, or spying on Arkansas, on Whitewater, on Paula Jones, on me. "Paranoia runs deep, into your mind it will creep," something like that from someone before. It's comforting to know you're never beyond the reach of DOD. In any event, no bombs were dropped, and we experienced no fireballs of collision with earth, only a return to the serenity of Mother Buffalo.

Sun and heat waned as we approached the largest island on the Buffalo at Arnold Bend. We went left and gazed in awe as the small flow of water met a multicolored ragged bluff at the turn back to main channel. It was simple, it was spectacular. Most special things and moments in life are.

That evening, just two bends below the Highway 65 bridge, we found another pluperfect campsite. Beneath a low-slung bluff, a forty-by-one-hundred-foot gravel bar offered a cool pool of deep green water and fresh feeder branches in which to bathe and wash clothes. I know, it's not environmentally sound, but we're filthy. I write as Ben

Arnold Bend.

Another perfect campsite.

cooks. Ben never cooks, but this meal is his; steak and beans, beans and steak, prepared by him personally. He did his homework, too.

As I watch him, I think of the routine we've settled into. We paddle hard through long slow stretches of water to reach our appointed daily quota of miles, fishing rapids and pools with good cover. We stop only for lunch, a snagged lure, a photograph of fish, or a quick dip. Sometimes we float for hours without uttering a word, each of us in his personal corner of a magical spectrum. We begin site selection for the night's lodging in late afternoon, or find the perfect spot prior to realizing that it's late afternoon. It just seems to happen.

I set up tent and bedding. Ben unloads the canoe and builds a fire. We bathe in the river. I nurse a drink and suck up silence and scenery. Ben does homework. We cook, we eat, and at dusk we are thinking about bed. We stoke the fire and pile on the big ones. We check the sky and retire to our tent and quick, instant, deep sleep. Such creatures of habit.

I awaken with dawn's light and reclaim the fire. First juice, then cereal, and then hot, strong coffee. Ben joins me, coffee the official start

Ben cooks dinner.

Homework time.

for him. He sits and stares while I repack the duffel. He loads it all. No one has assigned these tasks. It just seems to unfold this way.

Then we take another river bath. This is perhaps *the* moment, the peak of twenty-four hours: a slap of cold water that pumps heart, rushes brain, sears senses as you throw your body into the current and then soar skyward with a guttural gasp, the sun steaming the droplets and dowsing the chill. We are clean, awake, alive, tingling with energy and perhaps even the possibilities of the day—so different from the shaves, hot showers, suits and ties of home.

A friend, John Mike, once attempted to shave in concert with his morning river bath. He slipped around the bend from his fellow travelers, disrobed, lathered up standing knee-deep in the current, and stroked away the stubble. As he raised a small mirror to admire his handiwork, the reflection revealed three canoes coming around that same bend just seconds before he heard their gasps. As he plunged into frigid current to protect dignity and decorum amid the chuckled "good mornings," he vowed never again to seek the trappings of civilization on the river, or so he says.

Ready for the day, we push off, usually around 9:00 to 9:15 a.m. The river lies before us. The days and trees, the clouds, the colors, the bluffs and bends weave into one. To some it becomes a sameness, but never to me; rather, I experience a continuity, a subtleness, an evolutionary flow. I think I'm lucky.

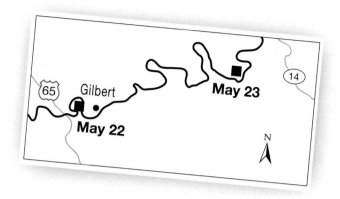

Day Seven: May 23, 1995
Past the Highway 65 Bridge to Spring Creek (18 miles)

I been walkin' on the ground,
waitin' for the pieces to fit.

    —Ozark Mountain Daredevils, "Standing on the Rock"

Today we stopped at Gilbert to load up on supplies and my dad talked to my mom on the phone for about two hours. I found a really nice dog, and played fetch with him for a long time. Shortly after we got back on the river, I caught a 2½ lb. Smallmouth which almost ripped the rod right out of my hands. I also caught a few other fish, but not as big. A doe ran into our camp and took a pee right in front of me. I got a good picture of her.

    —Ben's journal

    This morning I contemplate contact lenses and body odor: poignant observations about two disparate topics.

    First, the contacts. Without them, I'm blind, blind as a bat, blind as a log, blind as the rock I'm sitting here staring at. I have the kind you can wear for a week, but I've never done it. Therefore, I brought all of my paraphernalia: saline solution, cleanser, sterile rinse, and so on. It's day six on gravel, yet I've been afraid to clean them.

Hooked!

The realization—as I squat over a tiny mirror on the gravel bar and gingerly extract them one by one, place them in a small plastic cell, sleep without sight for a night, try to place them back on my corneas at morning light—that they might get lost, torn, or damaged during this process is causing me great anxiety.

What if I lose one? What if I scratch my cornea removing one? What if I tear one or both of these fragile fake eyes? Who will guide the canoe, who will pick campsites, who will read the sky for storms, who will pick the V on the rockiest rapids? Ben? Fourteen-year-old Ben P.? Yes, Ben. Besides, these lenses are beginning to scratch like the dickens. I don't worry about such at home in front of the mirror. Replacements are but a phone call away. Here, I could lose control of this critical part of my life, of my ability to see.

Homesick? No. More aware of my limitations, my dependencies? Yes. More in tune with the interdependence of two kindred souls in the wilderness? Yes.

As for BO, there's not much to say, other than that it's becoming a more noticeable part of me. Two river baths a day and clean shirts are powerless in its path. Do I miss deodorant? No. Do I recognize the impact of applying it each morning at home? Yes. Does it seem important? No, and far too much time has been devoted to it in this journal. Contacts and BO, BO and contacts—what more to say?

As we pulled into Gilbert, halfway through our journey, we touched again, at least in a sense, civilization. A quarter mile up the gravel road is an old general store, the only one on the entire 125-mile course, with cold milk, fresh ice—all those things cool that have slipped quietly away the past several days. The dry ice is history but served its purpose of keeping meats, breads, and other freezables frozen for future use.

Outside the store, I hesitated, then picked up the dreaded pay phone, the single instrument of comfort and civility I had not once missed, and dialed home, hoping things were OK. They were, but Betty was hassled: Patrick had missed going to the state tournament by a stride, Bart was about to be evicted from his new apartment, Patricia was on an endless toot, and Newt Gingrich was dating Barbara Boxer to save Bob Packwood's gavel. Betty sounded tired. I felt guilty, but after thirty minutes the warmth returned, the connection intact. I missed them all, excluding Newt and his buddies, immensely.

And then the call to work. This I dreaded. What more could have gone wrong? Who else had resigned? Any suicides?

When the trip was planned, I had a boring, dead-end job with an organization where bonds of loyalty had become a yoke. By the time we left, I had a new, exciting, and significant challenge to face. The opportunity couldn't have been better; the timing couldn't have been worse.

And though it had been easy to be up-front with my new boss about the importance of this adventure to my son and me, and equally expedient for him to bless it in every way, as the time drew nigh, the magnitude of my departing grew in proportion to the other challenges we faced.

It didn't matter that this was probably the only window for Ben and me, the spring of his eighth-grade year. It didn't matter that there would be enough water to float the whole course only now and that Ben would have little, if any, time to spare from school after this year. It didn't matter that the trip had been planned for two years, that Ben had earned it, albeit barely, and that school had blessed it. What mattered was the timing. I was facing a new job, a new boss, a new direction, a mass defection of employees and depositors, a need to comfort those who stayed, employees and customers, a need to reassure friends and former customers that I valued their business, a need to hire, from veterans to those who could simply answer the phone. I felt the pressure of keeping the doors open with half a staff, the tears of people pressed to their limit yet giving me the benefit of the doubt. The compression factor was immense—but I'm repeating myself.

Dare I go back, let alone call in, after leaving them shortly after joining them and creating all this chaos? I dialed with trepidation. The stress and tension were still there in their voices, but things seemed to be holding together. I felt a pang of guilt, and then I moved on, to fresh water, fresh rapids, fresh food, ice, and pursuit.

When we left Gilbert, two hours after arrival, I was comforted to know that the home fires still burned, and relieved that the bank doors remained open. Quite frankly, I was glad to get back on the river, to leave the real world behind. Now there's a slip—*the real world.*

This is REAL. The green I've seen under today's sun is REAL green— bright, alive, sparkling with spring. The blue I knew before this sky was drab and dappled with particles of soot and dust. The sun is a pure yellow here, unfiltered by contaminants of man. The air smells fair, sweet, and fresh. This is the REAL world, even if not quite as it was when my kin roamed these environs, when you could drink water from your hands. I had done that as a fourteen-year-old on the Buffalo, if only from feeder springs. It crossed my mind: what if our grandchildren could do the same? Would that define progress?

This world is REAL in the context of mankind's inventions, intrusions, and conveniences. I once knew what REAL meant. It is helpful to be reminded

The hills, bends, and horizon meld into one: sameness to some, continuity to others; a pale patchwork to some, a brilliant tapestry to others. I count Ben and me in the latter camp. We must never dull to the point of forgetting the difference.

We float past the remains of an old railroad bridge where once I camped with Ben, Patrick, and friends. We had told tales of ghosts and haunted gravel bars. I recalled suddenly walking off into the darkness as if in a trance, muttering about the infamous "Ghost

Train," while the boys hooted at me. Funny thing—they were all huddled together tittering nervously when I abandoned the charade and
ran screaming from the bushes into their circle of fire fifteen minutes
later. Ben laughed aloud as we thought back. Then we were past
Maumee with its long curving bluff.

We camp at Spring Creek this night, on a high gravel bar with running water but no bluff. Shame, shame on us. As we scavenged for
firewood, I heard Ben gasp. "Dad, look!" We had a visitor.

A doe stumbled out of the brush behind us and simply walked into
camp. We have heard deer, raccoon, and others at night, but this doe
was a little brazen. She seemed unafraid as Ben grabbed the camera
and clicked away. She ambled toward and then by me, limping
slightly, down the gravel bar toward the sinking sun. She entered the
water and swam to the far shore, scrambled up the rocks, and was
gone.

As we ate our dinner, we discussed her and the leg she dragged.
Ben felt she would soon be more than "gone." "The coyotes will get
her."

I watch Ben in the wild with wonder. His instincts, his comfort level,
his attention to detail—so unlike at home. His interests lie here. No
animal, noise, or rustle escapes his inspection. He says little. His
movements are few and effortless.

A campsite visitor.

Ben in his element.

When we've talked, it's often been about the beauty, the treasure of this place and time. We've discussed his indifference to socialization, to joining, to convention, and how that might help or hinder his future. He claims to be motivated and that his remarkable turnaround in school was in his own self-interest, not that of this trip. I guess time will tell.

We have talked about what he might do with his life. His science teacher says he is a scientist. We've talked about preserving this water, this valley, and others like it, for those to come. At times he seems to think he can't make a difference. At others he admits to the desire and need to try. He frames it in terms of catching a five-pound Smallmouth, or two or three of them in his lifetime, like Burl Cox, his hillbilly fishing guide icon. He senses that to do so in his life, and to share that wonder with friends or children, he must fight to preserve these hallowed places. He reasons that there should be stricter regulation of fishing takes, of river usage.

Watching him here next to me in the tent, big, bushy, at peace, gives hope to me for the rivers, Smallmouth bass, and sundry critters of the world. For, if Ben P. truly adopts their cause, violators best beware.

That night about 1:00 a.m., I was awakened by distant yipping and yapping, and finally a plaintive howl, the only such raucous ranting of the trip. I suspect Ben had been right about the doe.

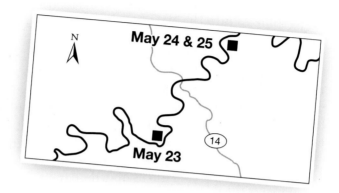

Day Eight: May 24, 1995
Spring Creek to Mid Rush (11 miles)

Better get back to the country,
'cause that's where we all come from.

   —Ozark Mountain Daredevils, "Standing on the Rock"

Today was a good fishing day and I caught about 20 bass. I saw another cottonmouth, and a different one before that. The river changed back to bluffs from the green hills. The bugs are really out and the mosquitoes are killing us. After seven days, this wonderful place is our new home, and I never want to go back.

   —Ben's journal

   Happy Birthday, Bart! I remember speaking to your mom on this day nineteen years ago. She had just baked you a cake, and I could hear you chattering in the background. Little did we know what a major part of each other's lives we would become.
   Eighteen miles yesterday? Unheard of. Almost an insult to purposeful piddlers like Ben and me. Four nights ago we were worried about the Friday noon rendezvous with my brother. Today we could reach it, if need be, a day ahead of time.

Mind you, there's a price to pay for rushing, even if it is to assure a timely arrival at Rush. No Hemmed-in Hollow, no Richland Creek, no standing astride The Narrows, no John Edding Cave—too many repetitions of "another trip" in this narrative.

We fish more today, and the fishing is excellent. Instead of lunkers we see many large, active bronze beauties. Probably a front is moving in. We float past Jackpot Bluff on the left, so named for the old mine that punctured its backside long ago. Then Stairstep Bluff on the right, to which I had trouble applying the given moniker. Maybe it looks more like stairsteps in the winter without the thick green tree cover.

Then we reached the Highway 14 bridge and a rumble from cars, not thunder. A couple spoke to us from the bank as we drifted by. They had traveled all the way from California to float the Buffalo and pressed us for information about different stretches. They longed for the twelve days we spoke of but had only three and wanted to invest them wisely. I suggested Ponca, and they nodded.

A mile farther we passed a low-slung rock formation on the left, almost but not quite a cave, washed out at high water by a sharp turn

Yet another "Brownie."

The bluff at Buffalo Point.

in the current. Four boys took turns sliding down the narrow chute. This was Buffalo Point, a major camping and National Park site. Around the bend, a smooth, whitewashed bluff bowed out from the top and stretched hundreds of feet—extraordinary.

We were but seven miles from Rush with a day and a half to burn. It was time to slow down and sniff the catfish, or something like that.

Evening's end arrives amid the clatter of thunder. I sit watching earth's ugliest creatures, buzzards, soaring effortlessly in union above the bluff dwarfing our gravel bar. They circle and glide, a battalion of scavengers that from this distance defines beauty and grace.

The weather that we have awaited all day moves in. A stalled tropical depression over Baja was one answer we received as we queried other floaters as to our fate these next few days. Another said the storm was flowing northeast and would only skim our turf. Thunder says it will do more than skim.

Ben sits reading *To Kill a Mockingbird.* It's an assignment, but one to which he seems to look forward more than the rest. For the most part Ben's reading consists of magazines such as *Missouri Conservationist, National Geographic,* and *Field and Stream.* He struggles with "textbook" material. Whether it's the content, a learning disability, or a lack of effort is unclear. I only know, particularly after this trip, that Ben reads and retains. But as with his writing and his drawing, what motivates him is a mystery—one that Mrs. Sermos, his science teacher, has tapped, and the rest of us haven't.

Apart from his nightly math sheets and journal entries, I have my own regimen with Ben. One course involves fish and fractions. Ben has made an A in eighth-grade math for two trimesters and yet hasn't a clue about basic fractions. Therefore, we measure each fish in eighths of a pound on this trip. It's not a pound and a half or a pound and a quarter, it's one and however many eighths of a pound. It's not three-quarters of a pound, it's six-eighths of a pound. Ben doesn't like this methodology, because it tends to diminish the size of his fish. Like all good fishermen, he rounds up. Still, he knows more than when we started. We are also memorizing lines from *A River Runs Through It.* He asks why, and I say because I admire them. He asks why we should memorize someone else's words, why not write our own? "Just do it" was about all I could come up with.

As if by magic, the vultures are gone, vanished as quickly and silently as they appeared. The bluff stands alone and terraced. Ben wants to climb it tomorrow. There is a grassy knoll halfway up, maybe a hundred feet. We'll see.

He'll need to wear boots if he goes. Snakes are everywhere. Ben had another moccasin encounter today, on a densely covered bank where he had snagged his lure. A large water moccasin sat poised to strike a frog a foot from where the lure was hung. We saw both only as he reached to free the lure. I don't doubt for a moment that had he followed through with his reach, he could have been hit. He wanted to hang around and watch nature at work. I could think only of getting clear of that bank, which we did.

Ben's buddy, guide Burl Cox, tells a story about a pair of moccasins. When a man shot one, the other stalked the man. Ben remembers that story. He's a bit edgy tonight.

Rain begins to move in. I hope it's not a lot. We're camped all right, about fifteen feet up, but a flooding Buffalo could stop us from completing our task. We've come ninety-five miles and have thirty to go. We do not want to come up short of floating the whole Buffalo.

Ben thinks this gravel bar is the best of the lot. It's long, high, and elliptical, with clear, swift water flowing like a moat between it and the facing bluff castle. The bluff is too broad for a picture or even an artist's palette, too dappled with color. It's an impregnable fortress of time and nature. I hope it protects us from the brunt of the blow tonight.

I dwell on one last thought as we slip into sleep. At dinner, as I poked at the fire, it popped and sparked into my eye. I felt a tiny burning sensation and watered through it. My concern heightened when the sting remained. Ben took a look and confirmed a red dot on the white of my eye, outside the contact lens zone. This should be OK with sleep, I reasoned, and it was. The could-have-been, a millimeter or so to the left, was another potential trip stopper. You're never home free, again. We take to our dry beds this eighth night, with gratitude and the threat of wet lurking.

The site for two nights of perfect camping.

Day Nine: May 25, 1995
Mid Rush (0 miles)

William Atrimity, he's a big waterman.

> —An old rhyme, source unknown, via J. Wyman Hogg, Ben's
> great-grandfather

Today we stayed at the same camp because we didn't have many more miles to make until we meet my uncle at Rush. The fishing was bad, and most of the time we just piddled around. My dad made me a great shore lunch, and I look forward to enjoying two steaks tonight. I caught a real pretty soft shell turtle. With the steak tonight we will have frog legs that I got.

> —Ben's journal

The day blooms wet and warm, definitely preferable to the wet and cold of earlier days. Befitting the moisture-laden air, fingers of fog creep between turrets of bluff overhead, imaging a Scottish castle or feudal manor.

It rained last night, hard at times, but not enough to raise the river. Nature's sponge, this large and porous gravel bar on which I sit, had already soaked up the wet bounty and is processing it for seepage into the river. We slept and slept and slept, through it all, from 8:15 p.m. to 7:30 a.m. I can't sleep like this at home. Too much noise, too many distractions, too much pressure, too little receptivity? Who knows.

Maybe it's the whippoorwills. Each night at dusk they start. Ben jokes that they've followed us yet another day. I counter that they are on or near every gravel bar in the world, and that if ever he notices a float evening without one, he'd better worry: worry about the water, the woods, the whole of nature's realm. I wonder if I'm right, and I hope he'll never have to find out.

Today we rest and piddle, which is what we normally do best. We once passed three days floating nine miles, inspecting every nook and corner along the way. That's today, because we're one day early.

This will be a source of wonder and disbelief for my wife. She still recalls the famous "midnight float" of the summer of '77. My son Bart, then three; my brother; our friend Don Deters; and me—the four of us out for a relaxing afternoon of floating and fishing on a stretch of lower Beaver Creek that none of us had ever set canoe on before. Not to worry, Parnell had a map, the fish were biting, and the beer was ice-cold. I had introduced Bart to floating earlier in the summer, but never without his mother at his side. We left the shuttle car downstream and put in at midday. Come dusk, there was no sign of the car, but it must have been just around the bend. Come dark, still no sign of the car, and the only light was from the moon. I'll never forget Bart, wrapped in a white towel to cut the evening chill, sound asleep, sitting on the cooler, silent like a small statue, even when we raised the lid for another frosty. Come 10:00 p.m., come midnight, still no car. Finally, at 1:00 a.m., we saw a log on a large gravel bar—our mark. We were elated that we had survived such a perilous journey, walking through rapids by feel rather than by sight, not panicking, not passing the mark. We were particularly proud of Bart. We (I) had erred significantly in our estimate of the distance of this float (it was twelve miles rather than six), but we had been resourceful enough to pull it out, to make ends meet. Right. We didn't exactly receive the hero's welcome we expected upon returning to my parents' house. Sleeping Bart was snatched from my arms at the front door by my bride, with nary a word of gratitude for bringing him home safely. My friend received a similar welcome from his wife. My brother was fortunately unmet and had only to endure the silent storm of the other two spouses. My dad called the sheriff to cancel the "all points" and managed a smirk or two. Only Bart could speak in our behalf, and he was dead to the world. We survived, marriages and all, and Bart even asked to go floating the next morning. Since he was still the only one speaking to me, I opted to scrape and bow for a while. But on this trip we're early, and that's cause for celebration.

Hopefully, the sun will dry us out today. We could stay and explore, or float a mile or two. What a nice dilemma.

We stayed, and what a beautiful day I had with Ben. He was in his element today. He grabbed a beautifully colored soft-shell turtle from the river bottom for a photo before releasing it. He fished, he hunted, he wandered at will, he explored, he roamed. As a result, we ate fresh goggle-eye for lunch and fresh frog legs for supper. His instincts and eyesight astound me. As we walked along a riverbank, wading the canoe upstream, he said suddenly, "There's dinner, Dad." He pointed

Eatin' well on the river.

Ben and a friend.

to a long hollow log, and as I stared into its depths I was greeted with two eyes in the dark. Snake, I questioned? "No, big bullfrog," claimed Ben. I wasn't about to test his theory, but when the shots rang out, it was indeed a large frog that hopped out, headless, his legs unscathed.

As we sit here now, preparing to cook those legs, Ben squats beside me skinning a large water snake for his science teacher, Mrs. Sermos— a hatband, he mumbled.* Do you think Mom would like one I asked? You think not? Good call. It is a beautiful skin, orange, yellow, and brown, with perfectly formed patterns. As he peels away the remaining flesh, he speaks of the musk that will disappear with drying. Ben, if only you can find a way to channel this focus, this energy, this expertise.

This is our last evening alone. Tomorrow my brother joins us with fresh food, water, and wine. Thoreau said, "You never gain something

---

* I subsequently learned that killing both the snake and the frog was illegal. While ignorance is a poor excuse, the lesson learned was valuable. Snakes are esteemed and respected by both of us now, even if they still scare me to death. And frog legs still taste like chicken.

but that you lose something," or something like that. I'll never lose the memory of this time alone with you, Ben. I'm much the better for it.

These nine days have flown by. My respect and my concern for Ben have both increased. My respect for his maturity, his many talents, his knowledge and love of nature, his ability to focus, to stay calm in difficult and challenging circumstances; my concern for his basic education, his lack of attention to detail, his willingness to say "I can't do that." To not know basic fractions at age fourteen is inexcusable. And before you ask why I took him out of school for two weeks if he's so deficient, I would note only that he knows more fractions now than he did two weeks ago. Perhaps more troublesome is his acceptance by default. "I'm not good at that" is more than a learning problem.

I talk to Ben of this, of the need to follow through, to follow up. "Dad, you're not perfect either, you know." Acknowledging this obvious fact, I ask him to expound, to specify those qualities he likes least in me.

"You chew too loud, it really bugs me," was a start. We both laughed out loud. "You don't understand eighth graders," he continued. We

Ben bags dinner.

Snake skinnin'.

both laughed again. "You're weird—a liberal hillbilly hippie businessman." I thanked him for the compliment, then wondered to myself if he meant that he was unsure of me, uncertain of my values. It warranted further discussion. "You don't fish enough. You could catch a five-pound Smallmouth." "You don't know how to use firearms." "You suck your teeth." "You take too many pictures of Patricia." And then, as if he was gaining confidence, "You're moody." "You're too critical." "You take too much crap from other people; you only fight with words." He stopped then, and we were both quiet. Ben is often very insightful.

Later, I sit and remember almost losing Ben at age nine on a riverbank during a late June float trip with friends and kids. I recall beauty, grace of nature, night and day. Clear water with turtles and fish, crawdads and frogs. Long and verbose stories around the campfire, each turn lengthened, each tale as well. The river—its peace, its power, its cleansing flow. The young alive and alert; the old feeling young. Later, the startling realization of risk, maybe more.

We camped that Friday on a small gravel bar. We pulled out at noon on Sunday and soon were more than we began—more aware, more grateful, more humble. My sobbing child, trembling with terror, was left with bruised ribs, shattered confidence, misplaced trust. Ben took the river for granted. He saw only its charm. More than that, I let him down, and dream about it yet today.

The water that Sunday was cold and clear—and high. As the adults unpacked canoes, Ben wandered next to a low-water bridge with large metal pipes channeling the water underneath. Prior flooding had created a deep dropoff at the bridge's edge. He stepped too close and was sucked into the mouth of the middle pipe in a torrent of foaming current. He screamed as he clung to the cement slab, his head barely above water, a nine-year-old body beneath the bridge, poised in a gaping hole of darkness from which he might or might not be spewed forth again if ingested. Ben recalls being whipped around, grabbing on, going under, pulling up, watching me move toward him in slow motion. He speaks as if time stopped for a moment or two. How he hung on as I ran on water to his side, I don't know. It took two of us to free him from that gremlin grip beneath that bridge. The end was not the shadowy recess of an underwater tomb, not entanglement in a web of limbs at the pipe's end, though it could well have

Ben with the old gray canoe.

been. A corner of my mind still chills at the thought, and occasionally screams in the night. I almost lost him.

I know Ben better after these days alone with him. I think I've gained some understanding of his strengths and weaknesses, not much different from what we had thought, but confirmed. Much work and opportunity lie ahead for Ben. I think he might be a "big waterman" in a true sense, not in the context of my grandfather's whimsical rhyme.

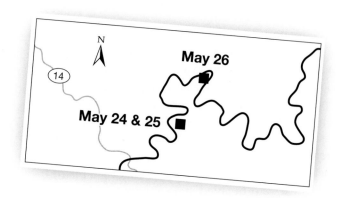

Day Ten: May 26, 1995
Mid Rush to Cedar Creek (4 miles)

_____

Sometimes it's better to travel than to arrive.

—Robert M. Pirsig, *Zen and the Art of Motorcycle Maintenance*

This is our 10th day of the trip and our 100th mile. We met my uncle and his friend, Barney, at Rush. We took off and camped about a mile down from Clabber Creek Shoal, across from Cedar Creek. The fishing wasn't too good, probably because it rained hard for about two hours. As we sat beneath a tree for shelter, I quickly fell asleep. When I woke up, the rain was gone and the skies were clear. We had a great dinner and I am very relaxed.

—Ben's journal

Finally, a truly wet day. It rained during the night, and it rained this morning, but still no rise. The falling drops broke for breakfast. We got most of our sleeping gear assembled and duffel-ized before they resumed their patter. An hour in the tent, punctuated by thunder and dripping leaks, brought home how fortunate we have been these nine days to not have had more inclement or dangerous weather. Being really *wet* on the river is no fun, and to date we've been spared that.

Ben reads Harper Lee amid the drips. He is attracted to Atticus. That's good, as I recall.

As my bowels rumble and moan in tune with the thunder, I finally can endure no more. For some reason, I began taking a large umbrella on float trips several years ago, to the jeers and taunts of my comrades. "Getting soft" was the weakest of their observations and, to be totally honest, I had never once found occasion to open it. At last my instincts were vindicated, no matter that only Ben was around to serve as witness. I ambled forth from the blowing tent into the wet and squatted in relative dryness under my much maligned umbrella—humbling, but functional. Thank you, Ben, for not taking a picture.

With the rain-delayed start, we paddled for most of an hour and pulled into Rush Landing at 12:05 p.m., one of the few times over the course of ten days that a timepiece was consulted. We were barely five minutes late. It is difficult to be on time from hour to hour amid the bustle and chaos of city and family, so arriving five minutes late after more than two hundred hours en route struck me as nothing short of remarkable. In fact, it was my brother who was late. It was good to see him and our friend Barney, with whom I've floated for twenty years.

Ben and I hitched a ride back to Dodd's Store to pick up ice, while my brother loaded his canoe. We rode through the old mining town of Rush, founded in the mid-1800s and inhabited as recently as 1960— a zinc mining settlement as I recall. Some of the buildings still stand, in ruins, and the mines themselves lie open to casual exploration. I wondered if Rush Creek is more or less polluted now as it tumbles down the rocks to the lower Buffalo than it was in those days of ore extraction and open sewage. I haven't a clue. The National Park Service maintains the area nicely now, and there is a haunting silence to it, broken only by trucks and the trailers of canoe liveries.

We shoved off and paddled a hundred yards to a high gravel bar on the right to scout Clabber Creek Shoal. Stories abound about this set of rapids, but it's really quite simple under most circumstances. At higher water levels, like today, the river runs straight and fast for fifty yards before sheering sharply to the left, and then back right. Large rocks line the right bank, but they are submerged today and present no threat. They do channel the current into a tight pattern producing significant haystacks. Every effort to bear left of the brunt of

Ben in Rush, Arkansas.

their cresting, particularly in a heavily laden canoe, is warranted. We slipped through with but a splash or two of cold water.

We were not so fortunate eighteen years ago, when my brother and I set off one midsummer's afternoon from Rush to introduce my new wife, Betty, to the charms of the lower Buffalo. The water was a touch lower, placing more of a premium on steerage. My brother bravely took our food, beer, and gear in his canoe. I took my wife. Because it was late afternoon and the large dinner sirloin was still frozen, he placed it on top of the cooler to thaw in the summer sun. As he entered the left turn, he clipped a rock but was able to right the canoe prior to disaster, except for the steak, which was lost into the depths, we presumed. Well, it would be potatoes and whatever fish we might catch over the next forty-five minutes for my wife's first gourmet river dinner.

Unfortunately, the fishing was slow, more like nonexistent, and as our stomachs began to grumble, we pulled onto a beautiful high bank of gravel to set up camp. As we unlashed our gear, I caught sight of a strange object drifting downstream, reflecting the setting sun. I glanced, looked again, and to my wife's dismay plunged into the

Clabber Creek Shoal.

Navigating the shoal.

water with glee. Had the pressure of marriage already caused me to snap, had I seen another woman, had she simply married a loony? I returned with the tightly cellophaned steak not only intact but perfectly thawed as well. This really happened, though my wife maintains to this day that she was duped. Rare meat never tasted better. Again, a true story.

Then there was the trip with my sixty-plus-year-old mother on this same piece of river twelve years ago over one long fall weekend. Mom. What can I say? She slept on the rocks with her two sons, helped drag the canoe (yes, the same Grumman) across low-water rocks, caught more and bigger fish than either of us, and claims to this day to have had "the time of her life." It's a family affair, this lower stretch.

More hard rain fell shortly after Clabber Creek, perhaps a forty-five-minute shower. Ben fell asleep in the bow, under a dripping tree, as the water fell on and around him. He was, as always, at home with nature's offering. I drank beer and spat sunflower seeds—and thought about the journey. I also thought about Betty, Bart, Patrick, and Patricia Jean. I looked forward to seeing them again.

Our Cedar Creek campsite.

Happiness is . . .

I used to drink beer, a lot of it, on float trips. Perhaps I will again. I did not on this one, not any during the day. But then, this was not a float trip. This was a journey, a pilgrimage. This was a quest not for relaxation but for something more. I used that word *quest* before and am still grappling for a context. I don't yet know what I really mean.

I do know that I felt a great burden of responsibility: for twelve days of safety, learning, and perhaps additional bonding. I know that there was little margin for error, or Ben and I would be miserable, perhaps even at risk. Some of these risks we had encountered despite every precaution: the moccasin episodes, the cold and power of the river from Ponca to Kyles, the burn to my eye. My task was to minimize risk and be prepared to respond soundly if things turned ugly—that didn't mix with beer.

We camp tonight across from Cedar Creek. We camped long ago as a family on this timeless gravel bar, high, moonlit, with water running in our ears. Tonight there's no moon, but we ate well: pasta with shrimp and butter garlic sauce, salad, something green for the first time in a week, and a rich Cabernet. We should sleep well, too, as the skies clear and the duffel dries. We are indeed returning to civilization, as we know it.

Pat took Ben fishing at dusk, and Ben returned an hour later with a prize in hand: a beautiful largemouth bass, his first of the trip. Thanks Patrick.

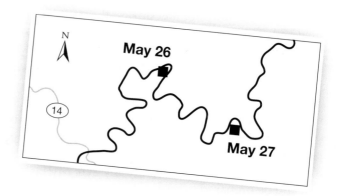

Day Eleven: May 27, 1995
Cedar Creek past Big Creek (11 miles)

Know what a light night is? It's a night that nights the light. How does
the night light . . . by making it darker.

—David James Duncan, *The River Why*

Tonight is my final night on the river during this trip. It will definitely be
hard to leave this river—it's becoming my home. But I know I'll be back
on the river soon, especially with summer coming up. We saw another
raccoon today, and my dad and Barney heard a bear grunt. The fishing
was good today, but most of our fish caught were small. I went back and
caught a trout in a creek [Big Creek], it probably swam up from the White
River.

—Ben's journal

A cloudy morning greets us. Thunder rolls. Not another episode
under the umbrella, I hope. While others sleep in, I sit with my cereal
and am again struck with the beauty, grace, and power of this valley.
With the bluffs farther up and back, the mountains begin to loom
larger. The river's waters spread, then are forced together at driven
spots. The current is exacerbated. We slept at the head of such a rapid:
loud, strong, pulsing with power.

While we pack, Ben prowls the mouth of Cedar Creek again, catching a few small ones. His silhouette, sun-filtered against the deep green of the shoreline, is cause for the rest of us to take note. We simply sit and watch for a spell, hot coffee in hand, beauty abounding.

Today, Ben floats with Patrick—two kindred souls, I think. They'll talk hunting, guns, rounds, and their respective love of the outdoors. Ben looks up to Patrick, and always has, staying with him in Branson over the years. I think Patrick admires Ben as well: his independence and simple, natural ways.

Wind is swirling today and hampers our progress. We are starting to see people again. Even on this remote stretch of the river, Memorial Day weekend spreads tentacles of humanity. There is nothing noteworthy to report about the scenery, except that it all is noteworthy. We walk up Big Creek to fish, and Ben catches our first trout of the trip, up from the White some twelve miles.

This evening, Patrick talks mostly about Ben. He marvels at his skills, in the canoe, casting a lure, seeking out wildlife. He speaks of Ben's passion for nature—why does everyone use that word *passion* with quiet Ben—and the need to nurture and allow its evolution. He's right. The alternatives are suppression or neglect, and in both cases I can see Ben turning to other things and people that offer less. Coddled, pampered, spoiled, ignored—No. Pushed, prodded, watered—Yes.

Patrick spoke also of my other Patrick. I mentioned earlier Betty's words of warning about his anger toward me regarding this trip, about his work ethic and his efforts to do his best each day without special treats or incentives, about his resentment of me for providing, and even pushing, this special opportunity for Ben. First Betty, then big Patrick, is warning me to listen, to understand, to compensate, to find ways to reaffirm my son's special gifts, his maturity, his responsibility. Don't be defensive, they say.

I know they're right on all counts. I love Patrick as only a father can understand. I sense our sameness in attitude, vision, approach to life. We share a focus on goals and objectives, a tendency to say yes and to believe when we should question more deeply, perhaps even a quiet moodiness. Not that he doesn't draw from his mother as well, or far exceed my skill set; but I see myself in his thought processes, his reason to be. I sincerely hope he can avoid the confusion this has caused me!

Ben working the mouth of Cedar Creek.

My brother Patrick and Ben.

Perhaps I'm too assuming of his success, too little concerned about his ability to function effectively in a compromised and materialistic world. In fact, I hold him somewhat in awe. Am I wishfully thinking about my own unfulfilled fantasies? I think not. He is simply the most mature and responsible young man I know. He is also my son, a dream come true, if I must place that burden on him. Will we be close? I pray we will. Can one be close to one so alike? I don't know. I am to my dad. Better not let him read this until I'm in the nursing home.

I think back to an episode gone by when I put him at great risk, when a father's wisdom caved in to carelessness. It was June of 1986—Patrick was eight; Ben, five—Father's Day of all days, to be exact, when this father made a bad call that could have proved deadly.

We floated Saturday with nary a hint of rain to come—my wife, the two boys, our old dog Coco. Sudden thunderstorms cut short our evening meal and overnight turned the Huzzah River to chocolate. By morning, the sun was hot, but debris and fallen limbs carried on a bed of brown water raced past our tent, perched high and safe on the gravel bar.

Our choices were simple: wait it out in the sun as the water cleared and began to recede, or ride the crest. As I said, Bad Call. I took Ben, only five, fearing him most likely at risk even with a life jacket, and turned Betty loose with Patrick and Coco. It took but two bends before I sensed my mistake. I took the lead in a dogleg rapid to test its difficulty. In turning to see them follow, I saw instead their canoe being carried into a newly downed tree, turned broadside against the green leafy barrier, deep brown rushing all around.

They clung to the wall of limbs, precariously in balance, for the time being. The slightest shift in weight would have rolled them into water-clogged tangles beneath the tree, and might have kept them there. Fortunately, the dog was scared stiff, Betty remained calm, and Patrick, at age eight, took orders well. I pulled to shore and ran back up the bank, leaving Ben confused and frightened. I crawled out along the tree to the canoe. It was then that I truly feared for their lives as, despite their calm, it became clear there was no easy way out.

I explained to Patrick that I would reach into the canoe, lift him free, and toss him into the roiling brown water downstream from the tree. I assured him that his life jacket would safely ferry him to the gravel bar and Ben waiting below. I promised to jump in after him.

Ben "desponding" by the campfire, our last night out.

I told Betty that I had no choice but to push the canoe, with her and the dog, away from the log, and that she must stay low and maintain balance at all cost. Once clear, she could go after Patrick. She reluctantly agreed that this was the only course. Coco cowered.

It all happened so quickly: pull Patrick, toss him clear of branches, shove the canoe to midriver, and jump in the water after him. At this point the dog abandoned ship as well—to rescue Patrick, the boys swear to this day. We all ended up safely on the finger of gravel below, the boys exulting, Betty mad, and me severely shaken. As we reboarded, and I swear this to be true, Coco slipped quietly into my canoe. She refused for the remainder of her years to ever again enter Betty's.

All this is to say that I'm an equal opportunity stupe when it comes to those I love most. It frightens, confuses, and even shames me, in that it is only on the river that I've had such lapses with them. I don't understand. I can only hope to do better with Patricia Jean, and be grateful for second chances.

In any event, I will try to deal with Patrick's anger and resentment in a constructive way and to find a means of reaffirming our bond and his conscientiousness, now and always. I am grateful to his namesake and my wife for raising my level of awareness.

Ben is beginning to "despond." Reentry will be difficult for him. He's quiet tonight. He sits brooding, staring at bluff, sky, ripples. He is separating.

He crouches now near the fire, in pitch dark, restringing his fishing line for tomorrow's last casts. "How can you see to tie the knot?" I ask. "You don't need light to tie a knot," he responds. There's something profound there, I think.

Day Twelve: May 28, 1995
Big Creek to the White River (11 miles)

We must all stand in the water,
we must find it when we roam,
it don't matter what is said
we can wake up from the dead.

—Ozark Mountain Daredevils, "Beauty in the River"

Today was my final day on the river for this trip. It was a beautiful day, but the fishing was the worst I have ever seen it. I didn't catch a single Smallmouth even though we didn't fish a lot. We got to the mouth of the river and people in motor boats were just all over the place. My uncle dropped his pole in 10 feet of water, and I had to get it.

—Ben's journal

This morning dawned cool and clear, washed from top to bottom. At 1:00 a.m., Mother Buffalo offered a parting kiss. A sudden, violent storm surged through the narrow valley below Woodcock Bluff, ripping our tent fly from its moorings and propelling it to who knew where. What we did know was that we would get very wet very soon without that cover. What we didn't know was that there were tor-

Last morning out.

nado warnings posted all along the Buffalo valley and north into southern Missouri.

Being the eldest and most infirm, I was nominated to chase down the roof to our shelter. In actual fact, I was the first one with shoes on. Flashlight in hand, I checked our canoes with fears of flash flooding in the back of my mind, then ran down the long gravel bar, becoming more concerned with each step.

I returned empty handed. And then I heard flapping on the upwind side of the tent, and there it lay, still attached by one cord, tugging at the ground. We were quickly and mercifully under cover again. As thunder roared and lightning raged, I fell fast asleep, never doubting that this too would pass.

I tramped down the same gravel bar at first light to photograph a fascinating fog bank, sucking up the first rays of sun. The day would soon be clear and hot.

We lingered in camp, Ben and I, not wanting to discuss the implications of this day. Then, after a last bracing river bath, we were off. Ben fished half-heartedly, silent for the most part. We passed fly fishermen bathed in morning sun, their lines glistening. Then Leatherwood Creek appeared on our right, feeding into a deep drop and a short rapid past a massive facing bluff, one of the last of the trip. The reflecting sun turned the water chalky green at the bluff's base. There were many campers about. But then again, this was Memorial Day weekend. Even though each gravel bar was taken, our fellow guests in paradise numbered in the hundreds rather than the thousands that would have descended on this stretch if it had been dammed twenty years ago.

I thought about that as we drifted past Elephant Head Rock, a potential dam site in the late 1960s. Dam site, damn site, whatever, we have all been spared, even the hordes who would have surely descended today had a concrete and steel water prison been erected on this spot.

Ben and I both laughed as we reminisced about Betty and Patrick breezing past an elephant without ears or tail. Ben noted that the eye sockets seemed deeper than he remembered them. Every view of each marvel magnifies our memories.

We continued to drift on, knowing our goal was at hand. We had passed the point of accepting journey's end and sensed completion, closure. We began to paddle toward the green hill ahead, knowing

Approaching the White River.

that the sharp right turn would lead directly to the mouth of the Buffalo, its confluence with the mighty White River.

The White—so central to the region's, and our family's, history and growth—forms in northwest Arkansas, flowing north into Missouri, then east through my homeland, Branson, Rockaway Beach, Forsyth, then again south into Arkansas, Flippin, Cotter (where Parnells and kin have lived for more than a century), and finally into the Mississippi via the Arkansas River, as one of its principal tributaries. Dammed here, dammed there, tame and docile, packed with people: Beaver Lake; Table Rock Lake, which Dad helped create; Powersite Dam, where my grandfather started his commissary business in the early 1900s; Bull Shoals; and Norfolk. I have read that paddle wheelers once plied these waters, even up the Buffalo, to fetch lumber and minerals, these same waters that we were coasting down.

The White, a mighty river, perhaps the greatest of all Smallmouth streams at one time, was brought to its knees by dreams of commerce, water control, cheap energy, and recreation. I'm sure there was a dollop of greed involved somewhere as well.

It was on the White River that Jim Owen of Branson pioneered the consumer "float trip," with float guide characters like "Little Hoss"

Jennings, Tom Yocum, Ted Sare, and the generation that preceded Ben's mentor, Burl. I recall a photo of my Aunt Pat in a *Life Magazine* article about Jim Owen float trips in 1941.

It was the White that cost my parents a child—a flooded float and capsized johnboat that resulted in my mother's miscarriage not long after I was born.

And then we were there. We saw the opening, fifty yards wide, maybe two hundred yards ahead, where Henry Schoolcraft had entered the Buffalo in 1819, one of the first white explorers to see her pristine waters and teeming wildlife.

It was an emotional moment for me, perhaps for Ben, as we eased into the cold, crystal-clear, power-generated current of the White. We high-fived with paddles, he grinning, sun streaming, water glistening, earth smiling. For a moment or two we were one: with one another, with our hostess of the past eleven days, with the ghosts of our past, with our destiny to float Mother Buffalo together, and, yes, with our need to move on.

A busy moment, I'd say. There have been few like it in my lifetime. One journey completed; another begun.

Journey complete.

Musings   Later 1995

So, why did we do this, Ben and I? What is the significance of floating the Buffalo, in total, all on one trip?

As I sit in the air-conditioning this evening of return, amid TV clatter, hot showers, and creature comforts, I still struggle for the right word or words. I know it was important. I don't know how to name it.

Were we out to conquer the Buffalo and stroke the ego? No way. She will never be conquered. Maybe crippled as we know her today—by government and corporate avarice, man and his minions. Maybe altered or rent asunder by an earthly eruption. But never conquered. The word simply doesn't fit.

Ben and I passed twelve days on the Buffalo River. We lived in her grace, free of harm, there for longer than most. We did not live off her, nor did our months of planning do much more than simply get us there. We served at her mercy.

In actual fact, we were lucky. Floods and tornadoes tracked one hundred miles north rather than straight down her gullet. We were spared nature's wrath and treated to her bounty, civility, and serenity for the most part—through no brilliance of our own.

Nonetheless, I sense that we both sipped deeply from the well of life's basics: of sky, blue or scarred with lightning; of green trees and water; of creatures whose life span is less than ours but whose species have far outlived our own. This dip into time brought meaning and, in a world of shift, provided a base on which to stand, from which to draw energy, power, and reserve.

We sucked as much from Mother Buffalo as we could. I sopped up her history, her beauty, her place in the flow of life, her legacy. I'm as full of her, and of what is sure, solid, and real, as I have been since my youth. In a sense I returned to my youth to find the river and my roots intact. Ben's portion of her potion will play out over the years. I'm sure he is better from this time and place.

So call it a quest, a pilgrimage, a seeking of shrine, a search for soul, whatever. However I frame it, we drew life, energy, and calm from what has been an eternal certainty in the lives of our lineage. Ben could say it better with fewer words. But then again, if he has the opportunity to return at midlife with one of his, he may grapple with what's inside as well.

Today is Thursday, June 9. It's 11:30 p.m. and I'm wide awake. I look back at today and recall two weeks ago.

Today, I awoke at 5:30 a.m., showered, shaved, ate cereal, and raced to the bank. I had three or four cups of coffee this morning, two cups with lunch, two this afternoon, six meetings, two interviews, more than twenty phone conversations. Tonight, I had a stiff scotch, a half bottle of red, and half of a beer while I watched the daily gore at 10:00 p.m. Tomorrow, I must be at work at 6:00 a.m. to prepare for an 8:00 breakfast, a 10:00 call, a 12:00 lunch, a 2:30 planning session, a 3:30 interview, a 5:00 civic duty, and, I hope, an evening at home with family. I put together Patricia's new Big Wheel tonight (not easy for a mechanical moron), learned of my brother's divorce trial, threw away a forty-eight-dollar bottle of medicine because my daughter couldn't swallow it, and learned that Ben's eighth-grade trip to Six Flags was marred by the arrest of three of his female classmates for smoking dope on the Screaming Eagle. I'm feeling tired again, after only two weeks.

I scratch the callous in the crook of my right hand where I cradled that paddle for nearly two weeks. It's peeling off and will soon be gone.

I touch the soreness at the outside of my left ankle where the fury of Gray Rock's rapids slammed me against a sunken boulder. The dark purple shadow and swelling have left. It will soon be healed.

I rub the dent on my left shin, first opened above Erbie and banged daily on canoe or cooler with each exit to walk a rapid or skirt an obstacle in favor of maintaining a dry duffel. The indentation will likely stay with me, a small reminder.

I lie in bed, but sleep won't come. The distant roar of an airplane fades to the hum of the alarm clock, the buzz of the baby monitor. A siren squeals trouble to the south and fades into a background clutter of TV from elsewhere in the house.

There's running water, but it's a toilet. No crickets or frogs, no current splashing rocks and gravel, no animal cries, no whippoorwill.

Two weeks ago at this time, I was sound asleep. Mr. Whippoorwill was alive and well, at least I presume he was, since he was going strong when I faded off with the sun at 8:45 p.m.

Ben and I had spent a memorable day of isolation, staying on our perfect gravel bar, paddling and walking a mile upstream to fish, once in the morning, again in the afternoon. Ben had stalked fish, frogs, turtles, snakes, and the bluff across the stream. We had enjoyed the fruits of his labor for lunch and dinner. I had tried to soak it all up but was simply not porous enough.

Two weeks ago, I slept ten hours, breathed fresh air, used mind and senses to observe and experience wind, rain, sun, animals, and my son. I was alive! Tonight, I'm tired. I look forward to five hours of sleep instead of ten. I miss the whippoorwill. I take some comfort that he is singing on some gravel bar somewhere. I miss his night-song here. I won't sleep well or long tonight, or probably the next.

Father's Day, Sunday, June 15. We come full circle this nineteenth Father's Day of my life, merely nine since the circle was almost broken on Huzzah Creek.

Patrick and Ben (and Spike the dog) took off on their own a few moments ago to float and camp overnight. It's not that they didn't want old Dad around, they simply wanted to do it themselves—at least that is what I tell myself. Nor did I help much with their packing. I did point out the need for a grill on which to cook the meat they had just packed, and that it would be helpful to have aluminum foil for the potatoes. But, like it or not, they really didn't need me.

I admonished them to take care, camp high, and come back to old Dad. I stopped short of telling them how important they are to me, but not by much. We called my dad before they left to wish him a happy Father's Day. He seemed pleased they were going. He may have thought back to times he had said the same. Ben and Patrick, Todd and Pat, Todd and Betty, with Bart and even Patricia, Mom and Dad—all separate but equal through bonds of time, river, love, and lore.

As they pulled out, I thought about that. Betty said, "Strange feeling, huh." Strange, but good, strong.

Father's Day. So many thoughts and memories. Patricia Jean chirps from her bedroom. Maybe she and I will pay a call on Mother Buffalo together some day.

I worried a bit about the boys during the next day at work. Upon returning from lunch with a client, I found a message waiting. "1:50 p.m. Boys are home. Spike ate all four steaks—Betty." Guess they didn't need the grill after all.

Late August. I read to Ben from the *Post-Dispatch* of two twenty-five-year-old former neighbors who had floated the entire length of the Missouri River. They had put in the very same weekend we had and were just now arriving with tales of history, snakes, rapids, dams, and water. I asked if we should do that next. He thought out loud, "90 days, 125 miles—I'd rather take three months and float the Buffalo a mile and a third a day." He has a point, and his fractions are getting better.

Fall. Patrick asks me to float the whole Buffalo with him next spring after graduation. But that's another story.

Acknowledgments

I must conclude by thanking Neil Compton, Kenneth Smith, the Ozark Society, and their many allies for brave efforts to preserve the Buffalo River as a free-flowing magnificent marvel of nature and a testament to the Creator's palette. Without them, there would be no Buffalo River, only another manmade lake drowning all but the upper reaches of an unparalleled watershed. And without the Buffalo River there would have been no story to plant between the pages of this book.

It wouldn't have happened either without the patience, encouragement, and understanding of Ben's mother, Betty, who accepted this dream and pushed to see it realized.

Ben has spent the better part of the last four years puttering around beautiful Swan, Bull, and Beaver Creeks in southwest Missouri, counting critters and assessing water quality, first as an undergraduate at Drury University, then as a graduate assistant at Missouri State University. Thanks are due to his mentors at each school, respectively, Dr. Steve Jones and Dr. Dan Beckman.

Thanks, too, to Sandy Sermos, Ben's middle-school science teacher, who assured us that "Ben is a scientist" at the lowest point of his pursuit of this dream.

Thanks to proofreaders Dr. Frank Reuter and Peter Parkhouse, who took a lonely manuscript and added focus, order, and polish that it might appear in readable form to you.

Special thanks to my friend Leon Combs, businessman, author, and Upper White River Basin Foundation board member. Leon inspired me to share this personal saga and provided the glue to create a story line.

And thanks to that grand old Buffalo River man Burl Cox, who recently passed away, leaving a storytelling void that may never be filled.

And with sincere gratitude to John Dillon and the Ozark Mountain Daredevils, whose music was such a poignant part of this story. We listened to them as we headed to the river then, and do still today, the relevance of their lyrics undiminished over time. All quotations are from The Quilt Album (1973), their first.

And, of course to you, Todd Benjamin Parnell—there would be no story without you. Thank you for taking your passion for things natural and committing your course and future to that interest.

Student Ben in the field prior to graduation.

But then again, that's another story.